D0370559

CO-017

A COMPLETE INTRODUCTION TO

GARDEN
PONDS

COMPLETELY ILLUSTRATED IN FULL COLOR

When the plants are full-grown, a man-made garden pool will look like one found in nature.

*The choice of plants,
especially those with
flowers, can improve an
otherwise ordinary rock
garden and pond.*

A COMPLETE INTRODUCTION TO

GARDEN PONDS

COMPLETELY ILLUSTRATED IN FULL COLOR

A small school of Japanese Carp blends well in this garden pool done in a typical Japanese motif.

Al David

Photography and Artwork

Special thanks are extended to Scott Boldt, John R. Quinn, and Mirko Vosatka for color drawings; to Dr. Herbert R. Axelrod, Dr. Sylvan Cohen, Michael Gilroy, Hanseatic Verlag, Kodansha Ltd., Charles O. Masters, Laurence E. Perkins, Dr. H. Reichenbach-Klinke, Fred Rosenzweig, Harald Schultz, Glen Takeshita, Edward Taylor, Van Ness Water Gardens, and Ruda Zukal for individual photos; to Aquarium Pharmaceuticals, Inc., Rolf C. Hagen (U.S.A.) Corp., Penn-Plax Plastics, Inc., and Wardley Products Co. for product photos. Lilypons Water Gardens provided the photos of garden pond construction.

Distributed in the UNITED STATES by T.F.H. Publications, Inc., 211 West Sylvania Avenue, Neptune City, NJ 07753; in CANADA to the Pet Trade by H & L Pet Supplies Inc., 27 Kingston Crescent, Kitchener, Ontario N2B 2T6; Rolf C. Hagen Ltd., 3225 Sartelon Street, Montreal 382 Quebec; in CANADA to the Book Trade by Macmillan of Canada (A Division of Canada Publishing Corporation), 164 Commander Boulevard, Agincourt, Ontario M1S 3C7; in ENGLAND by T.F.H. Publications Limited, 4 Kier Park, Ascot, Berkshire SL5 7DS; in AUSTRALIA AND THE SOUTH PACIFIC by T.F.H. (Australia) Pty. Ltd., Box 149, Brookvale 2100 N.S.W., Australia; in NEW ZEALAND by Ross Haines & Son, Ltd., 18 Monmouth Street, Grey Lynn, Auckland 2 New Zealand; in SINGAPORE AND MALAYSIA by MPH Distributors (S) Pte., Ltd., 601 Sims Drive, #03/07/21, Singapore 1438; in the PHILIPPINES by Bio-Research, 5 Lippay Street, San Lorenzo Village, Makati Rizal; in SOUTH AFRICA by Multipet Pty. Ltd., 30 Turners Avenue, Durban 4001. Published by T.F.H. Publications Inc. Manufactured in the United States of America by T.F.H. Publications, Inc.

Contents

Introduction

Ponds have been a popular garden feature for centuries, with clear evidence of artificial ponds dating back to the time of the ancient Egyptians, over 5,000 years ago. Today it has never been easier to construct a pond and incorporate other water features, such as waterfalls, into the basic design, free from the restraints imposed by the use of concrete. Other durable and more versatile materials have now largely supplanted the need to rely on this traditional means of providing a water-tight enclosure for a garden pond.

A pond can be designed to fit into any setting, either modern or traditional. It can be planted with a wide variety of plants, while fishes of different types afford an ideal means of providing color and activity in the water itself. Around the perimeter of the pond, rockwork may be used to form the basis of a rock garden, and the whole scene can be floodlighted for maximum enjoyment throughout the warmer months of the year. Although climatic constraints may dictate the types of plants that can be safely left outside during the colder months of the year, alpines are a popular feature of many waterside settings and, as their name suggests, tend to be very hardy. Even in temperate climates, therefore, a pond can be an attractive garden feature throughout the year.

After being built, modern ponds require very little maintenance, and no constructional expertise is necessary. All the necessary components, along with the plants, fishes, and other accessories, can be purchased from many pet stores. Since ponds and water-gardening generally tend to be regarded within the trade as seasonal, the largest selection of materials is likely to be available through the warmer months of the year. Before setting out to purchase the components, however, draw up a plan of the site and decide upon the type of pond that you want to construct in the area concerned.

Right: *Garden pools are particularly attractive during spring when most of the flowering plants are in bloom. Perennials will survive winter and bloom every year when properly cared for.*

Planning Your Garden Pond

THE SITE

Within reason, you can build a pond in any spot, but certain localities will be better than others. A site relatively close to the house is preferable, especially if you want to incorporate features such as fountains that will rely on a source of electricity being available. Positioning a pond beneath a stand of trees is not usually considered ideal, since this will tend to restrict the light and leaves will tend to accumulate and stagnate in the water over the winter. Plant growth in the pond is likely to be poor if the site chosen is excessively shady, so a sunny position is desirable.

A fairly sheltered locality will also assist in improving the appearance of the pond. Litter, including leaves, will be less inclined to pollute the water, while the plants growing around the perimeter of the pond will be stunted or damaged by being in an exposed, windy position. The site needs to be accessible from all sides, especially if the area of water is to be relatively large, which is desirable. A large pond needs less maintenance and is more satisfactory in all respects than a small pool. It is also preferable not to put a pond in a spot where it is clearly evident from the road, as it could serve to attract vandals.

Try to plan the pond so that it merges into the existing landscape of the

A series of paving stones provide a safe access for feeding and watching the koi in this garden pond. Koi watching is relaxing and provides some moments of retrospection in the hurried tempo of modern life.

garden. This is especially important if the shape of the pond is intended to be informal so that it does not clash with existing garden features. The pond is best located at a low point in the overall layout of the ground, since this is where a natural accumulation of water would be anticipated. An existing hollow can make an ideal starting point for construction purposes. It also provides scope for expansion at a later date, since a running stream or even a waterfall may be easily added without upsetting the natural balance of the scene.

Above; *In this design the small islet at the middle of the pool is conveniently reached by a wooden bridge. A hedge and evergreen trees create a natural-looking setup.*

Below: *A small fountain greatly improves the appearance of this otherwise simple garden pool.*

As always, a degree of compromise will probably be inevitable in deciding upon the most suitable site. It may be possible, for example, to adapt the existing landscape to some extent by planting a screen of fast-growing conifers some distance away from constructed, you can gain some idea of the appearance, relative to the rest of the garden, by marking out the site. Stakes connected by rope can be used for this purpose, or a trail of sand may be laid around the likely borders of the pond.

the pond in order to provide shelter from the prevailing wind. One of the great advantages of the new methods of building ponds is that they can be used to create a wide diversity of shapes suitable for virtually any chosen location.

While it is impossible to gain an accurate impression of how a pond will alter the scenery of the garden until it has been

A bank of evergreens strategically situated behind this garden pool in Japan provides the needed protection from possible strong winds and exposure to too much light.

Similarly, new access paths if necessary can be marked out in an identical fashion to give some appreciation as to how the appearance of the garden will be changed by the construction of the pond.

THE DESIGN

Ponds generally can be divided into one of two basic categories, and if their design is inappropriate the resulting effect can be disastrous even if the site itself is eminently suitable. An informal pond, for example, will not fit well into a formal garden, and it is no coincidence that ponds incorporated into such gardens at stately homes correspond in being of fairly rigorously defined geometrical

A type of garden pool befitting the back of a large property. A most natural effect is created by the sloping sides, totally bereft of any retaining wall. Wild birds are specially attracted to such a pond and may have to be discouraged by some means.

shapes. In this way the pond complements the design, form, and structure that have been created in the remainder of the garden. Ornaments and fountains are associated with ponds of this type but look totally out of place in a more natural and informal setting.

Within the average garden there is scope for either a formal or informal pond. A formal pond, for example, can be easily fitted into a patio setting, while informality in design is ideal for a pond intended to complement an area of rock gardens. Construction techniques may vary depending upon the type of pond that is required, while the use of plants will also reflect the pond's design. In the informal situation, for example, plants will be used to disguise the pond's artificial outlines, whereas this feature is emphasized and highlighted in the formal pond, reflecting its geometrical design.

RAISED PONDS

While in most cases the pond will be constructed in a pre-dug hollow irrespective of its design, a raised pond may be more appropriate in certain circumstances, especially if there are young children around the home. They will

The underlying framework of this raised garden pond is totally hidden from view by a series of large flat-topped rocks. Three pieces that are arranged in tiers provide easy access to the pool itself.

inevitably be attracted to a pond in the garden but are clearly at risk if they fall into even a relatively· shallow area of water. This is far less likely to happen with a raised pond, because instead of standing on the edge children will actually be peering over the structure. Their curiosity to see into the pond can be fully met, while the elevated height affords them protection against overbalancing and slipping on a wet rock at the edge, for example, since they are well below this level.

A raised pond is also more suitable for the elderly, since they can enjoy a better view of the pond without fear of losing their footing. A pond of this type may sound highly artificial, but it can be easily incorporated into an area of raised flower borders edging a patio, for example, and should not appear at all out of place under such circumstances. Most raised ponds tend to be of formal design, but this need not be an essential feature.

PLANNING CONSIDERATIONS

Formal ponds need to be located in a sheltered spot if a fountain is

A garden pond built in two levels. The smaller upper pool can be utilized for keeping fish intended for breeding, or perhaps those that are quite small and need special attention.

incorporated into the design. Wind can play havoc with the jets of water emanating from a fountain and may even cause a noticeable water shortage by blowing the spray outside the confines of the pool, especially if the area concerned is small. Water clarity also tends to be more significant in a formal pond, which may dictate further expenditure on a filtration system once the construction process is underway, although this is really a personal decision. Another factor that will have a distinct bearing on the clarity of the water is the depth of the pond itself. Algal growth tends to be more profuse in shallow water.

In addition, temperature changes are likely to be more marked in a small volume of water, and this can be particularly significant during the winter. Even with an air temperature well below freezing, ice formation is unlikely to extend for more than approximately 18 inches below the water's surface. Fishes will congregate in deeper holes at this time, and here the hardier varieties should be able to survive quite adequately until warmer weather returns, enabling

This rock garden includes a raised small and shallow pool that empties into a lower pool. Obviously, this type of construction entails some expenditure and heavy labor.

them to return to shallow areas. In order to overwinter fishes safely, therefore, the pond needs to be constructed so that it is at least 3 feet at its deepest point.

Apart from the fishes, the needs of plants must also be considered in designing the interior of the pond. Water-lilies tend to need a minimum of 18 inches of water, yet other popular aquatic plants will not survive at this depth. These others are commonly described as marginals, and it is usual, in order to reconcile these conflicting needs, to incorporate a "marginal shelf" around the perimeter of the pond where this group of plants can be placed. The maximum covering of water above the marginal shelf should not exceed 9 inches if these plants are to thrive in the pond. The breadth of the shelf Is also important since most aquatic plants are set in special pots within the pond, and these will need to fit comfortably on to the submerged ledge.

17

Aim to construct a relatively large pond with a surface area of at least 50 square feet so that you can incorporate a good selection of plants and fishes can be kept safely in an adequate volume of water where they will not

Left: *A row of paving stones serves as the edge of this pond. They are placed without mortar, simply resting on the ground. It will not prevent rain water from emptying into the pond.*

serve as a magnet for local cats and even passing birds such as herons. A small pond is likely to prove a source of heartbreak in every sense!

PRE-FORMED PONDS

The most immediately appealing option is undoubtedly the molded, pre-formed pond, which simply needs to be buried

in a suitable area of ground. These are now available in various materials, including plastic and fiber glass, and can be obtained in a wide range of shapes and sizes. Unfortunately, many designs are too small to be really satisfactory and are inadequate in terms of their depth. The marginal shelf in some cases may also be too small, so this type of pond has various drawbacks that may not be immediately apparent. In addition, these ponds are not particularly cheap, although at the end of the season they can often be obtained at a bargain price as the store aims to clear its surplus for the winter. The durability of these pre-formed ponds is a reflection of the material used in the construction process, with flimsy plastic units being easily damaged while those of fiber glass or polyester are far more rugged, a difference that is also discernible in their prices.

POND LINERS

The pond also can be constructed using a suitable layer of waterproof material placed in a hollow and filled with water. The edges of the liner, as in the case of the pre-formed pond, can be disguised using either paving stones or plants. However, cheap plastic sheets not specially designed for ponds are the least suitable material for construction purposes, although they are readily available. This is perhaps best reserved for ponds where there are no fishes, since water can be lost quickly from a leak in the liner, which is likely to be fatal for fishes, whereas the plants will survive for a longer period of time out of water.

Plastic pond liners tend to perish around the rim, where the material itself is exposed to the sun's rays. The ultraviolet component of sunlight attacks the plastic, causing it to become brittle, and ultimately it will crack. There is no way of overcoming this problem, although you can buy ultraviolet resistant plastic, which tends to have a slightly longer lifespan than its untreated counterpart. While clear plastic sheeting can be used, blue sheets are most commonly used for ponds, although once the pond is filled with water the color of the plastic assumes little significance.

It is not possible to repair plastic sheeting satisfactorily, and once it has perished the only option is to empty the

This garden pond is being filled by means of a garden hose; if the hose were elevated above the level of the water it would do a better job of aerating the water being put into the pond.

pond and replace the liner, which is a time-consuming task. Depending partly on the area concerned, the potential lifespan of a liner of this type is unlikely to exceed two or three years.

A more expensive yet satisfactorly option is provided by the use of a PVC liner. Two grades are usually available, of which the plain PVC sheeting is

The installation of a statue transforms this simple garden pond into a formal type. Such a statue is intended for garden ponds and equipped with an inner pipe for delivering water into the pool.

the cheaper. A reinforced variety incorporating strands of nylon is considered more durable and should last for perhaps 15 years or so. The PVC liners are laid in an identical manner to their cheaper polyethylene counterparts, but only a single rather than double layer will be required. They are less likely to be inadvertently punctured. Repair of PVC sheeting is possible if it becomes damaged. Various colors are produced; the darkest available, which will serve to reflect light back from the depth of the pond, is to be preferred.

While for many people PVC liners are quite adequate, the most long-lasting material currently available in this field is undoubtedly butyl rubber. It may well remain intact for half a century or even longer. Like the other forms of pond liner, butyl rubber provides a very flexible means of constructing a pond and is an easy material to work with, being quite suitable to form the base for a small stream, for example, connecting two separate ponds. It is available in various thicknesses, with .0 3 inch being favored for pond construction generally.

Working out the area of liner required and its cost is quite straightforward. First decide upon the width and length of the pond at its broadest points. Then

to both of these figures simply add a figure that will be equivalent to double the depth of the finished pond to give the dimensions of the liner required. It is usually sold in terms of area and priced accordingly.

As an example of the above, consider a pond that is to be 10 feet maximum in length and 5 feet at its broadest point. The depth will not exceed 4 feet. The overall width of liner required will therefore be 5 + (2x4) = 13 feet, whereas the length necessary for the pond will be 10 + (2x4) = 18 feet. This means you would need a liner that is 13 feet long and 18 feet wide. It is

A sprinkler type of water fountain can aerate the water to a limited extent. Note the absence of water plants in this pond intended for displaying ornamental fish only.

possible to join butyl rubber sheeting together if necessary by using a special glue, but this should be viewed as only a last resort, as any patching is a potential source of weakness for the future.

USE OF CONCRETE

While pond liners and even pre-formed ponds are relatively easy to install and require little maintenance, this does not apply to a concrete pond. Once in place a pond of this type is impossible to move, and subsequent expansion can be difficult.

In terms of materials and labor, a concrete pond will not prove a cheap option, and there is an increased risk of leakage with ponds of this type unless they are well built. Problems can result from the presence of lime in the concrete, which will dissolve into the water poisoning both fishes and plants in the process unless it is removed or coated adequately

The selection of garden decorations is wide – birds, frogs, seals, to name a few. These items together with the materials for constructing this small pool are available commercially.

A well built concrete and tile pond for keeping koi in Honolulu, Hawaii. For protection against strong light, one side of the pond is partially shielded by a simple roof.

beforehand. This again tends to be a laborious task if the pond has to be repeatedly filled and drained.

Although other means of constructing ponds can proceed in most types of weather, the building of a concrete pond always needs to be undertaken with a watch on the likely weather conditions. A heavy period of rain can ruin attempts to concrete the base of the pond, while overnight frost can be equally harmful, causing the newly laid mortar to crack. Even hot sun can be disadvantageous leading to too rapid evaporation of the water in the mix so that the concrete becomes dry and flaky.

If you do decide to opt for a concrete pond, therefore, it may be better to construct it during the late summer so that these problems are less likely to arise and the lime can leach out into the water before the spring, when the pond is drained and stocked with fishes and plants for the first time.

The first actual stage in the construction process is to mark out the site accurately using stakes joined by a rope. Then cut away the turf with a sharp spade if the area chosen forms part of an existing lawn. The turf can be kept and may be useful for landscaping purposes once the pond is completed. The cut turf should be rolled up and stacked on a flower bed or similar site out of the way.

Above: *The area to be dug is delimited by a rope or any other cord-like material. The ground being quite even, it is not necessary to use stakes.*

Below: *With the greater part of the pond's center already dug, the marginal shelf is carefully contoured along the edge of the pit.*

PREPARING FOR THE POND

Excavating the site for even a small pond will mean that there is a considerable surplus of soil available, and some thought should be given to disposing of this beforehand. It can of course simply be deposited in a rented dumpster and taken away by a commercial carter. If this is to be the case, arrange to carry out the excavation over the course of a day to minimize the cost of hiring the carter.

Alternatively, you may be able to use the soil elsewhere in the garden, especially if you plan to construct a rock garden. In this instance first remove the top soil, which accounts for the upper few inches of the earth, and keep it separate, since it is the most fertile part and ultimately can be redistributed over the new site. While the pond can be excavated with a spade, it may be preferable to rent a small backhoe for the purpose. This will at least speed the process considerably by removing the bulk of the soil, with the final touches being carried out with a spade.

It clearly will not be possible to dig an exact hollow to correspond to the shape of the finished pond, but try to cut the marginal shelf carefully, having marked this with an inner area of string. Once the level of the earth has been excavated down to the required depth for the shelf over the whole area, it is then preferable to actually start digging again in the center of the site, moving outward back toward what will become the marginal shelf. In this way the earth should become quite well compacted around the perimeter before the shelf is actually cut, so there is less likelihood of it collapsing. If this happens, however, try to minimize the effect and if necessary insert shuttering at the vulnerable points. It is

Above: *To prevent the collapse of the marginal shelf, the soil should be compacted and its level checked by a spirit level.*

Below: *Instead of having a pond with sloping sides a second shelf is created in the construction shown here.*

For stability the walls of the shelves are kept at a slant, not vertical, and the soil compacted further to create a solid and smooth surface.

Appearance of the just completed garden pond. Children and housepets are best kept away from the pond at this stage.

important to check that the floor area is flat, using a spirit-level for this purpose.

LINER POND CONSTRUCTION TECHNIQUES

Any slight irregularities in the surface will be dealt with at the next stage in the construction process, since a layer of sand with old newspapers above will need to be spread over the whole base. This will also ensure that the liner is not damaged by sharp stones or other projections once the pond is filled. Take particular care to remove any tree roots, however, since these may push up

and, over a period of time, can actually penetrate a liner. A layer of sand about 2 inches in depth will suffice, although at some points it may need to be deeper to compensate for any unevenness in the base.

The liner itself should then be set roughly in place, with its edges evenly supported around the perimeter with blocks. Take care when placing the liner within the hollow not to damage the sides of the marginal shelf. Indeed, try to avoid entering the pond base at this stage. It is useful if someone else is on hand to lower the liner in from the other side of the site.

Once the liner is in the hollow and evenly distributed, the pond can be carefully filled by using a hose. The weight of the water will serve to force the liner into the bed of sand, ironing out any creases in the process. Both PVC and butyl rubber are flexible materials, and therefore it will not be necessary to allow for any extra around the edges, although this does not apply in the case of polyethylene, where an additional foot will be required for this purpose.

As the pond fills with water the weights around the edge can be carefully removed, keeping it balanced so there is no tendency for a corner to slip down, for example. Then, once the water level reaches the top of the pond, the liner can be trimmed back as required by using a sharp knife, leaving a maximum of 18 inches exposed. This may then be weighed down with a layer of earth and turf applied on top so that it corresponds to the existing level of grass over the rest of the lawn.

Alternatively, the liner can be buried beneath paving stones or slabs with

A small amount of water will keep the liner in place. The liner is then arranged to follow the contour of the pond closely.

With the pond completely filled with water, the liner comes in close contact to the bottom and sides of the pond. The liner is pushed down along the marginal shelf and trimmed

mortar being laid on top to anchor the edging in place around the pond. This paving should be designed to overlap the edge of the pond slightly, since it will in turn help to disguise the liner where it leaves the water.

A PRE-FORMED POND

The initial phase of construction is similar to that required for a liner pond, although in this instance you can plan the site accurately simply by inverting the shell and, using either an edging tool or a spade, marking the boundaries around the shell itself. While this may be relatively straightforward, the actual excavation phase in contrast requires considerable precision and is not always easy, especially with a relatively ornate design of pond.

In the first instance, excavate the hole to a sufficient depth to ensure that the shell sits comfortably in position and does not protrude abnormally above ground level. It will rise slightly once full, but if it appears too low at this stage, simply remove the shell and add to the base using either sand or soil that is compressed into place.

Upon completion of trimming the liner, most of the hard work in constructing a garden pond is half over.

The weight of the paving stones keeps the liner in place and from shifting. Mortar is then applied to secure the paving stones on top the liner and to each other around the pond.

With paving stones in place and the water raised to the proper level, the liner is effectively hidden from view.

Potted water plants and floating plants in place, a simple fountain, a pool decoration, and you now have a very attractive garden pond.

The flat head of a rake can be used for this purpose. Then, using a spirit-level mounted on a piece of wood if necessary, ensure that the shell is positioned correctly, lying flat in position. A poorly laid pond will ultimately prove unsightly, so every effort must be made at this stage to ensure that it is level in all directions.

Inevitably, given the shape of many pre-formed ponds, there will be areas where there are gaps around the base; these must be filled in with either sand or soil. Judicious use of a trowel can be helpful at this stage, while a hose may be necessary to wash soil down into such areas if they are essentially inaccessible. Alternatively, back-fill the site by digging a sloping hollow broader than the outline of the pond once it is settled on the floor of the hollow. The soil can then be firmly packed back around the undersurface of the shell. Finally, the soil around the perimeter can be replaced as required, bringing the level back up to the top of the pond.

The weight of water in the pre-formed shell is likely to cause some expansion, but this will probably be only slight in

the case of a fiber glass pond. Provided that they are adequately situated in the first place, these ponds will not actually move. Again, the edges can be effectively disguised by the use of paving stones slightly overhanging the edge of the water.

A RAISED POND

The construction method required for a raised pond of this type presents slightly different problems, although clearly there is no need to excavate a large area of soil. The site will need to be marked out accurately and leveled. A solid base is required because of the weight of the pond once it is full, and it must be supported on the sides in order to prevent any weakness

A raised pond is desirable in a family with children, or where the substrate is not easy to excavate. The edge of this pool is broad enough to sit on, too.

becoming apparent in the form of a split resulting from the water pressure.

The top soil should be removed to a depth of 8 inches and a solid layer of hardcore used as a base on which a 4 inch slab of concrete will be laid. This will provide support for the pond, preventing subsidence once it is full, as is otherwise likely to occur if it is stood just on the earth. Check that the concrete is level, so that the pond itself will stand on a flat surface. The sides of the pond are best disguised by a wall that can be of stone, brickwork, or blockwork as desired. If the pond is to form part of a raised border around a patio, for example, then the same building material is likely to prove desirable throughout.

The border can be constructed to fit directly under the top edge of the pond or may be built to fit flush with it. It may be desirable to fill the gap between the wall and the outer perimeter of the pond with concrete to provide additional support. This will lessen the

raised pond of this type stems from its outer casing, and for this reason the services of a skilled bricklayer could prove a considerable asset during the construction phase. The top of the pond can again be disguised with paving stones of some kind set in place with mortar.

BIGGER STRUCTURES

Larger raised ponds with any individual measurement exceeding 8 feet will require additional reinforcement. The base

The edge of a pool can be raised to any height desired. Here two layers of roughly hewn blocks of stone secured by mortar are used.

likelihood of the wall being cracked by the water pressure emanating through the structure of the pond once it is full. Part of the appeal of a

should be several inches more in thickness, and welded mesh laid in the concrete will serve to prove additional support for the great weight of water above. An extra thickness of concrete around the sides may also be recommended. Any undue pressure at a

Constructing a cobblestone section at one corner of a common oblong garden pond results in less common pond configuration. For a natural setting plantings of some sort are necessary.

vulnerable point is liable to cause the pond to split and start leaking, so considerable care must be taken during the construction phase. As an alternative to concrete for back-filling, sand can be poured down the sides to fill gaps that later could develop into pressure points.

CONCRETE PONDS

In technical terms, the pond liner affords probably the easiest means of construction. While some professional assistance often may be needed when constructing a raised pond, it is likely to prove essential if you opt for a concrete pond but have little practical building experience. You can minimize the likely difficulties by opting for a straightforward design in the first place.

Whereas the site for the pre-formed pond corresponds essentially in size to that of the shell itself, being just slightly deeper to allow both for any rise in the height of the pond and for a covering border around its perimeter, this is not the case for a concrete pond. You will need to allow for a layer of concrete that will be 6 inches in overall thickness when it is completed, so that either a smaller pond or more digging will be the result. Perhaps the sole advantage of concrete for pond construction is its immediate flexibility. You can alter your design as you build the pond, which is not possible with the pre-formed shell and not very practical with a pond liner.

A concrete pond is labor-intensive, though, and it has to be built in stages. Reinforcing mesh will also be required and should be incorporated during the initial phase. Gently sloping sides will facilitate the construction

Above: *A bilevel type of garden pond is most appropriate for a sloping terrain. The flow of water is easily controlled by blocking the opening between upper and lower pond sections.*

Below: *In this illustration, a section of the brick wall is deleted to show the precast shell within. This type of pond obviously requires a strong and level foundation, otherwise the shell could buckle and crack.*

process, avoiding the need to rely heavily on shuttering to hold the concrete in place at the edge of the pond. The base itself, including the sides, should be well-compacted so that it will not subside later once the pond has been completed, as this could cause the concrete to start leaking.

The whole of the interior should first be lined with a double layer of heavy duty polyethylene as an additional precaution to protect the concrete from losing water too rapidly into the soil as it dries and against leakage in the long term. If the water escapes into the soil, this is likely to cause the concrete to dry too quickly and can lead to premature cracks and

A figure-eight configuration is achieved by placing two circular pools together. The series of stepping stones, the waterfall, the small resthouse, and plants at the background invoke a rustic impression to this design.

weaknesses being introduced to the structure at this stage.

Shuttering if required need not be elaborate, with plywood fixed to a wooden framework being ideal for the purpose, provided that it can be adequately supported. Struts running from one piece of shuttering to another may well be necessary.

PREPARING THE CONCRETE

Even for a small pond, a relatively large volume of concrete will be required, so the renting of a mixer for this purpose is likely to be advisable. Apart from being quicker and saving considerable effort on the part of the builder, the machine should also ensure that the sand, cement, and gravel are properly mixed. You may be able to purchase ready-mixed concrete direct from a vehicle, but this might have to be moved a considerable distance from the road to the site of the pond, which is extremely exhausting work. Since the load will probably have to be booked several days in advance, there is also no guarantee that the weather will be favorable when the load actually arrives.

If you do opt to mix the concrete yourself, use three units of gravel to two of sharp sand and one of cement. These can be simply poured into the mixer, but when preparing the concrete by hand do not add water until these components have been thoroughly mixed—the presence of water makes this task much harder. In any event, water should only be added a little at a time so that the resulting

concrete does not end up loose in consistency but is nevertheless clearly moist. This should help it to stick to the walls, although the plastic lining may actually prove detrimental in this regard, necessitating the use of shuttering.

As soon as the concrete is in place, lay the mesh on top and gently press it into the damp concrete. The reinforcing mesh does not need to be of a particularly heavy gauge—19 gauge chicken wire, for example, is quite suitable for the purpose.

Right: A very formal type of garden pond. Nothing irregular in its design, of uniform symmetry and components.

Check with a level that the base has a roughly even covering of concrete and pat it down well to remove air bubbles that could later become a source of weakness. A board can be used for this purpose. A second layer of concrete will then need to be applied to a depth of about 2 inches to cover the chicken wire totally and increase the overall thickness still further. This can be applied subsequently, after the first layer has begun to dry out. The surface in this instance should be smoothed over by using a plasterer's trowel if it is to form the permanent inner lining of the pond. Wetting the tool at regular intervals will help to ensure that a good finish is obtained. Any shuttering used should be removed before this final coat is applied.

A major danger, especially in warm climates, is that the concrete may dry out too fast. This can be prevented by carefully draping damp burlap sacking over its surface. It is likely to take several days to become firm, and this process should not be rushed. Apart from the risk of cracks developing there is also the possibility that the surface will tend to flake off if the water evaporates very rapidly. The only option under these circumstances will be to apply another coat of concrete and afford it more protection from the sun.

Some builders of concrete ponds like to use a third different cement mixture to form the surface layer. No gravel is used in this instance, just a combination of three parts of sharp sand to one of cement with a waterproofing substance also being included in this final stage. The second coat can be reduced by about 1 inch in thickness as a result.

A decision will have to be made as to how to deal with the potentially toxic release of lime from the newly laid concrete once it comes into contact with water. It is possible to fill and then empty the pond repeatedly at weekly intervals over the course of the winter, for example, checking the water chemistry using a special

Right: *A series of rocks arranged on a sloping terrain create the channel for the flow of water into a raised pond. The plants in the surrounding terrain are typically temperate for this pond is situated in the United Kingdom.*

pH test kit available from most pet stores. The other option is to neutralize the effects of the lime before it can gain access to the water. This can be carried out by painting the sides and base of the pond with a suitable sealant. Various treatments of this type are available, some of which require a primer. The danger is that, unless the treatment actually neutralizes the lime chemically, the covering may become damaged, causing the seepage of

A tropical setting is created in this garden pool by goldfish, water-lilies, and ferns. The gentle flow of water from the waterfall scarcely stirs the pool water allowing a good view of the fish.

lime into the pond at a later date, with potentially catastrophic effects on the occupants.

IS IT WORTHWHILE?

Building a concrete pond is undeniably hard work and also proves costly, even if you do not actually employ someone to help you. To gain some idea of the likely

Paving stones are the most recommended material for edging a garden pool. Available commercially, not too heavy to lift, they can be installed manually using the most basic hand tools.

expenditure before starting work, you can estimate the cost of the basic materials by first calculating the area to be concreted and multiplying this by the depth of cover. An average bag of cement holds about 1.25 cubic feet. Allow for an additional 25%, since the overall volume will be reduced by an equivalent amount once water has been added.

EDGING AROUND THE POND

While turf can be laid up to the edge of the water, this is often not satisfactory even around an informal pond. Muddy patches will inevitably develop sooner or later, and it is difficult to cut the lawn without bits of grass falling into the water. As an alternative, a variety of paving materials can be used to create different effects corresponding to the type of pond, with stone paving often being popular for this purpose around an informal pond.

The site around the pond

Instead of flat stone slabs, large boulders are utilized for edging this garden pool.

irregular slabs of stone. These should be positioned in place on a bed of concrete and tapped down to ensure the surface is level. A slight slope of the slabs away from the pond can be useful, however, especially during wet weather, since rainwater and any overflow will need to be prepared, being dug out and leveled if necessary. Paving stones with a regular outline will be easier to lay than

from the pond will drain away over the paving rather than simply flooding the surrounding area.

Stone paving requires less skill to lay successfully than do other materials. It is possible, though, to surround the pond with brick paving, creating an attractive patterning. This can prove tedious around a large pond, but the result will be durable, provided that hard bricks are used for the purpose. These will not be attacked by frost. You may be able to obtain a large quantity cheaply from a demolition contractor. In this instance, however, the bricks will probably have to be cleaned, with old mortar needing to be chipped off before they can be laid again.

Irrespective of the pattern to be created, start by defining the perimeters of the path, laying the borders first. Then fill in from the edges, using the natural dimensions of the bricks as far as practical when planning the size of the overall site. It is possible to obtain bricks in different colors so that an attractive contrast can be incorporated into the paving if required.

Tiles are rarely used for edging purposes around a

A natural garden pond is possible in places where the water table is not too deep. Marsh type plants can be grown at the edge of the pond and floating and submerged water plants in the pond.

pond, simply because they are expensive compared with other materials. A range of colors and patterns is available, however, and tiling can be incorporated alongside these more commonly used paving materials. Check that any tiles will not prove slippery, as these are liable to prove dangerous close to the pond.

DRY BEDDING

Tiling is best set permanently in place on a bed of mortar, although this need not be essential, certainly with paving slabs. The important point in both cases is to ensure that the base is firm. Dry bedding entails the spreading of sand over the surface of the soil, with the paving being laid on top. Unless the base is firm, however, the paving will soon become uneven and potentially dangerous. Grass and weeds can rapidly become established between the slabs, so the area may need more maintenance than in the case of mortar-bedded paving. In this instance, mix sand and cement in a ratio of 3:1 and set the slabs on top, filling around the gaps between the paving stones.

The raised edging of this pond consisting of closely abutting paving stones create a smooth path for walking. Having no plantings in the pond, utilizing a single but strong sprinkler type of fountain enlivens the scenery.

GRAVEL

A gravel path around the pond is an easy option to prepare and maintain, especially if there is a double layer of polyethylene beneath. This will help to stop weeds from becoming established, spoiling the overall appearance of the intervals. Small plastic tubes cut to size can be disguised in the borders and will enable the bulk of the rainwater to drain away. Alternatively, small

The plastic sheet liner of this garden pond is covered by a layer of soil and gravel in which rooted water plants grow directly, as if found in their natural habitat.

path. Dig out and level the area, placing the sheeting down and constructing the borders of the path.

The main drawback of including the plastic is that it will prevent drainage of rainwater into the subsoil. It will therefore be necessary to incorporate drainage points at the base of the borders at regular holes can be made in the plastic to facilitate drainage. A fairly coarse grade of gravel is to be recommended, and the path can be leveled simply by raking it over the prepared site to a depth of several inches. This should prevent water from settling in puddles on the path even after a heavy rain.

POND APPARATUS

The borders of the pond may also be required to conceal electrical wiring, pumps, and other apparatus. Fountains are an integral part of many ponds, for example, but require a power supply. It is particularly vital to seek minimum depth of 18 inches. Clearly, the closer the pond is to an existing supply inside the home, the easier and cheaper it will be to provide an external source of electricity to power fountains and other equipment.

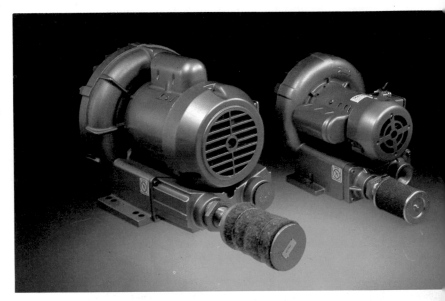

the assistance of a qualified electrician when running wiring out of doors for any purpose. There are in fact legal requirements that have to be met in this regard, and although these do vary, the safety of those who may come into contact with the wiring is of paramount concern. Any cables running out of doors must either be attached to a wall or else buried in the ground to a

The size of the pond determines the type of air pump to install. You will need to consult your local dealer and builder for technical matters about pumps and electrical equipment.

Lighting around the pond can transform the scene at night, and on a patio it ensures that you can dine out on fine evenings, being able to enjoy the tranquil surroundings of the pond at the same time. Apart from lighting around the

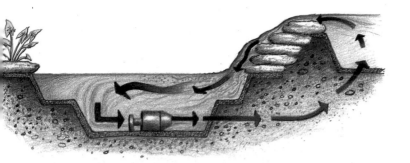

pond, it is also possible to include floating lights on the water itself so the jets of a fountain can be emphasized. Such lights can be obtained in various colors and filters can be fitted to some designs so that the actual color produced may be varied as desired.

Clearly though, the combination of water and electricity is potentially dangerous, so ensure that the lights are suitable for the purpose for which they

A schematic design showing the placement of a pump and the direction of waterflow in a bilevel garden pond.

are intended and are not damaged in any way. When purchasing such units, check on the availability of spare bulbs. Remember to use only submersible lights in a pond if they are clearly intended for this purpose.

This small (2 x 3 m) construction can be called a summer garden pool. If situated in a temperate area, it should be emptied in late fall or early winter.

FOUNTAINS

It is not difficult to set up a fountain in the pond, but clearly this will be much easier if there is no water within. A fountain can disrupt other pond life, however, and thus may not be ideal in every instance.

For example, water-lilies will only thrive under conditions where there is little water movement and will not do well in a pond

Shown are two types of fountain water outflow, a mushroom- or umbrella-shaped and a jet or sprinkler type.

Submersible pumps for operating water fountains. The different types of spouts are also interchangeable.

containing a fountain unless the area is extremely large so they can be set far away.

The most important component of the system will be the pump, which operates the fountain. The submersible type is most suitable for the average garden pond. Various models are available, all of which operate below the surface of the water, with their working parts being sealed in a water-tight casing to exclude water. Submersible pumps differ with regard to their capacity, some being more powerful than others. It is important to select a model that will carry out the task for which it is

required. Seek the advice of a reliable dealer for your individual needs. The height of the fountain required has a bearing on the pump, and in turn this will depend on the area of the pond, since water can be easily lost from the pool if the fountain is too big.

The submersible pump will need to be firmly set on a base in the pond so that the chosen fountain head is located just below the surface. Numerous types of fountains are available, and the choice depends essentially on

A decorative type of fountain in two tiers. Shallow basins store water temporarily before flowing into the small garden pool.

personal preference. It is simply connected by tubing to the pump. A solid bed of insoluble rocks should be laid in the pond to support the pump. This can be stood on a piece of slate laid horizontally, for example, but take care to ensure that the whole structure is solid. Never use limestone rocks or concrete blocks for this purpose, since these will adversely affect the water chemistry over a period of time.

The actual height of the fountain can be adjusted, depending upon the flow of water. A reduced flow, pumped through under greater pressure, will yield a relatively high jet of water. It can be difficult to adjust a fountain attached to a submersible pump once the pond is full, since this can only be achieved by wading into the water.

This difficulty does not arise with the surface pump, since it must be housed out of the water in any event. These pumps tend to be considerably more powerful than their submersible counterparts, and as a result they are better suited for use in large ponds, where they can operate other features, such as a waterfall, as well as one or more fountains.

An external pump needs to be located near to the water in a secure waterproof housing, which normally entails the construction of a special pump hose. Valves are responsible for controlling the flow of water through the pump, and a suitable arrangement will ensure that the pond can be emptied using this type of pump.

The water uptake tubing in both types of pump must always be covered with gauze, in order to ensure that fishes and debris from the pond are not inadvertently sucked through the system, where they could potentially cause a blockage. It is preferable with a surface pump to fit a cutoff valve to ensure that the pump will not empty when the power supply is cut off. This can also be done by putting the pump below the water level alongside the pond, but be sure that the housing is waterproof, especially the lid of the box, as it could be flooded here.

Right: *A variety of plants lends a natural appearance to this garden pond with a bridge across and decorative fountain head. Unfortunately, the wire trap for collecting debris is exposed to view.*

A variety of ornaments are frequently included in a formal pond, and they may have a provision to feature running water. A simple submersible pump will be adequate to operate such ornaments, which are connected together by means of piping held in place by clips located close to the pump outlet and the ornament inlet. It is always worth checking that the ornaments are not made of mortar if they are to be exposed to the water. In the same way that a chemical reaction will occur to liberate free lime in a newly built concrete pond, a chemical reaction will also result from the contact of such ornaments with water. The problem can be overcome in this instance by immersing such figures in a bucket or trough containing a 0.5% solution of household vinegar (a half part per hundred parts of water) and leaving them in soak for three or four days. Then rinse the figures off thoroughly and allow them to drain before placing them in the pond itself.

Right: *A large display of decorative structures for the garden or garden ponds. Those intended for use in a fountain are already equipped with an inside metal tubing.*

Filtration Systems

While aquarists keeping fishes in tanks in the home rely on some kind of filtration system to keep the water in a good condition for the fishes, this does not often apply under pond surroundings. Some fishes, notably koi, will benefit from the presence of a pond filter, however, and of course, the water will be clearer as a result so the beauty of the fish will be more readily apparent. The relatively sparse setup of most koi ponds, in view of the destructive natures of these fish, means that less natural filtration is taking place. Algal growth, which can be curtailed by an adequate filtration system, thus may become a major problem.

Commercial pond filters operating on the same principles as those used in the aquarium setting can be obtained without difficulty, although they tend to be expensive. It is more usual to opt for an external or submersible pond filter rather than an undergravel unit that covers the floor of the pond and is thus relatively bulky and cumbersome.

You could construct an external filter at low cost, operating it off a pump, but you must ensure that this will be adequately powerful for the task. A series of connecting chambers made by using plastic pipes cut to size and sealed with silicone aquarium sealant would be ideal for this purpose. They connect with each other by means of fine plastic tubing running from one compartment to the next, so that the water drains from the first chamber right through the series. Drill holes in the top of the pipes so as to ensure maximum passage of the water from one filter bed to the next. Each is filled with a progressively finer filtration medium in sequence, starting with coarse pea gravel. As the water flows through the filter progressively smaller particles will be removed. On the final passage, through silver sand, algae will be left behind in the filter bed so that cleaner water will be returned to the pond. The exit point can be arranged so that the outlet is directly into the pond. There is no need to leave the filter beds uncovered. Indeed, they

Right: *The choice of low plants in this rock garden is most appropriate. Tall plants would have hidden the small pond totally.*

can be effectively disguised as part of a poolside seat with a brick casing. The filter media can be changed when required without difficulty. Indeed, one of the key points to consider when purchasing any filter is the ease with which the unit can be serviced.

from the risk of free lime affecting the water chemistry, the presence of chlorine in the water itself

Below: *A garden pool that is deceptively so natural in appearance. These man-made concrete rocks, upon exposure to the elements, become overgrown with moss and algae.*

CHECKING THE COMPONENTS

Once the pond has been completed and the equipment installed, the system should be checked for any faults. Any adjustments will be more easily made in a pond without plants or fishes present at this stage. Indeed, it is not safe to introduce fishes to a newly filled pond because, apart

will prove deadly. Only a minute trace of chlorine needs to be present; concentrations of as little as 0.1 mg per liter can be fatal to fishes.

Right: *Water-lilies grow best in calm water. Thus, strong flowing water should be avoided, or these plants will be pushed into one side of the pond, crushed, their foliage ruined. Water forced by high pressure into powerful jets from a fountain is inappropriate.*

core of this type. Clay-based soils rapidly become waterlogged compared with those on a bed of sand or chalk. The center of the site should again be excavated, with the resulting hole being filled with coarse gravel or clinker, for example. The water will congregate here without harming the plants, while the soil can be added back on top.

The basis for the rock garden—and a factor that will have a distinct bearing on its character—is the stone chosen to form the contours of the site. The major cost of the blocks of stone will be transporting them, so it makes economic sense to opt for locally quarried stone where available. It may be inadvisable to choose limestone for an urban environment where there is likely to be any significant degree of pollution in the air, since the pollution will react with the surface of the limestone, causing it to become unsightly. Visit your neighborhood supplier before deciding upon the choice of stone, although obviously you should first have an idea of the plan for the rock garden before deciding on the stone.

Adequate planning is

vital when constructing the base, since blocks themselves will be very heavy, weighing perhaps as much as 2 tons each. An orderly design is to be recommended, with stonework being used to form terraces rather than being scattered haphazardly over the site

in individual pieces. It is essential that the blocks are firmly seated and evenly arranged. Some types of stone are easier to divide than others; sandstone, for example, can usually be cleaved without difficulty by using a hammer and chisel for the purpose.

A formal Japanese garden pool. This garden and pond will require regular maintenance, plants trimmed of excess growth, weeds pulled from between boulders, slippery algae and moss scraped, and the like.

If you intend to build a path through the rock garden to the pond, concentrate on preparing this first, as it will facilitate overall access to the site. In some cases the raised area of a rock garden may be utilized to create a waterfall. If this is anticipated, lay the necessary pipework once the base of rockwork is in place, before covering the area with soil. Once the rock garden has been completed, it will be much harder to undertake this task, so make an allowance during the construction phase for expansion at a later date.

Once work has been completed the existing earth can be replaced, but although the top soil will probably be useful in some areas, it may be necessary to prepare a simple soil mixture more suitable for the plants to be used. Alpines generally need well-drained surroundings, so the addition of grit to the soil in any event is usually advisable. Peat

A view of a small raised pond with fancy goldfish; a couple of bubble-eyed goldfish are recognizable. This variety requires some care and is not for beginning garden pond owners.

moss or adequately rotted garden compost is also useful, acting as humus in the newly constituted soil. As a general guide, equal parts of grit and humus should be added to an identical quantity of top soil and mixed thoroughly. You can alternatively purchase a suitable compost, but this will prove costly particularly for a large area. Brush off the stones once the soil is in place so that the site looks as tidy as possible. Keep the soil level within the constraints of the rock outcrops so that it will not be washed away when it rains, being spattered over the stones in the process.

MORE ELABORATE PLANS

It is of course possible to expand from one pond to another if space permits, linking the two together by means of a waterfall or simply incorporating this latter feature as part of an existing setup, using a rock garden to form the basis of the necessary gradient.

WATERFALLS

The construction of a waterfall is relatively straightforward, since molded sections can be obtained for this purpose without difficulty. Although

Koi, Japanese ornamental carp, is hardy enough to withstand a strong flow of water like this waterfall. Note the absence of any floating plants here.

these may not appear instantaneously attractive, they can be set into the ground and carefully disguised with plants, ensuring that the units remain as inconspicuous as possible while the flow of water is unaffected. Water should run over the sections in such a way that there is no risk of debris being deposited into the pond by the waterfall nor a risk of erosion of the bed. Indeed, for these two reasons a "natural" waterfall is unsuitable. It is vital to bed the artificial sections down carefully, ensuring that they are level, as in the case of sectional ponds. A pond liner can be used as an alternative means of constructing a waterfall, but the result may be disappointing, depending upon the flow of the water, if it appears too unnatural.

The waterfall can often be fed by means of a submersible pump that is also operating a fountain at the same time. Check that your model can undertake both these tasks simultaneously. Care must be taken when planning

Right: *The construction of a small reservoir along a steep incline of this man-made waterfall slows down the flow of water into the garden pond proper.*

the waterfall to ensure that the inclines are not too steep, otherwise water will be lost by splashing out of the pond. Another restricting factor to consider is the volume of water in circulation at any time. Water in the pipework and traversing the waterfalls will have been removed from the pond itself, and this could have a detrimental effect on the water level.

from a lion's head or a similar ornament mounted on the wall. A semicircular pond set against the wall can be linked to one above, with water cascading down and being pumped back into the top unit. Take care to ensure that the walls are able to withstand the water pressure and are coated to prevent the passage of free lime into the water.

OTHER OPTIONS

There are various other ways of circulating water, apart from a waterfall. In a formal setting, for example, water can be pumped from the pond, pouring back into the pond

A very formal piece of construction in Italian style. The component parts are usually available commercially. The small semicircular pond is sufficient for keeping a few goldfish. This type of pond is drained for the winter time; frozen water expands and possibly can damage the masonry.

FURTHER PLANNING

The scope for ponds within a garden is immense. Even in a very limited area, a special fountain can be incorporated successfully. The base can be constructed either of a pond liner or of concrete with a grid of wire mesh placed above. A brickwork perimeter above this then ensures that a bed of selected pebbles can be placed on the grid to disguise it, while access for a submersible pump and fountain unit is incorporated into the base unit. The low jet of water will then proceed to rain down over the pebbles back into the reservoir beneath, maintaining the cycle. Obviously, no fishes or plants are featured in this type of unit, which is

The placement of stones across a natural waterway can result in a small garden pond. This is perhaps too shallow, temporary in character for keeping any fish and it can possibly dry out during the summer.

ideal for a small patio. It may even be arranged in a semicircle.

Whatever you decide to construct by way of a garden pond, the inclusion of a water feature of this type affords considerable scope for further development wherever your interest lies. The best thing of all is that modern technology has ensured that building a pond and other water features can be undertaken with confidence even if you have no previous experience in this field.

Planting Your Pond

The plants typically found in ponds can be divided into a few basic categories: *Oxygenating plants* are found within the main body of water and are especially significant for a pond containing fishes. Although they will liberate some oxygen into the water during hours of daylight, the major role of the oxygenators as a group is to provide a spawning site where the eggs of the fishes will be deposited and remain until hatching occurs. The protective leaves of the oxygenators also help to disguise the eggs until they are due to hatch. *Water-lilies* are extremely popular pond subjects and, in common with other *floating plants* that spread over the surface of the pond, help to improve the environment for fishes and the overall appearance of the water. These plants provide shade for the fishes and enable them to forage for insects at the water's surface. They also serve to decrease the amount of light entering the water, which in turn will help to restrict algal growth within the pond. Algae are responsible for the problem often described by pond-keepers as "green water." The final group of plants likely to be encountered in a pond are the so-called *"marginals."* These, in contrast to water-lilies, vary widely in their appearance but will all thrive in conditions of shallow water. Some may naturally inhabit marshy ground but will nevertheless survive well in a slightly deeper area of water.

Pond-keepers also frequently incorporate marginal plants into a bog garden, which in practice can be a variable overflow for the pond itself. A small area of pond-liner can be incorporated below the existing level of the pond and planted with marginals. Providing that the area is not allowed to dry out, such plants will thrive equally under these surroundings as well as in the pond itself.

The following is a selection of the plants commonly available, along with cultivation details. The ideal time to introduce plants into a pond is during the late spring or early summer, since they will be entering their active growth phase at this time. If plants are not obtained until late in the year, the likelihood of establishing them successfully is reduced, and they may

Biological balance in a garden pond is possible with the right choice of plants and type of fish. Too many plant-eating fish can destroy plants and too much vegetation can deprive fish of living space. A happy medium is, however, possible.

simply rot over the winter.

Specialist aquatic nurseries stock the largest variety of suitable plants for the pond, but the average pet shop catering to garden ponds will be able to supply a good

selection of suitable plants that are usually container-grown. The main benefit of the specialist supplier will be evident if you are searching for a particularly rare or unusual water-lily, for example. Under these circumstances you may have to purchase by mail-order.

Never leave a plant in its wrapping longer than necessary, but remember that aquatic plants are especially at risk from desiccation and should be kept moist at all times when out of water. Although the plant itself may not by killed by being allowed to dry out, damage is likely to be evident on its leaves, which will spoil its overall appearance.

It is important to treat all aquatic plants before placing them in a pond that will also house fishes. This is because both parasites and disease can be easily introduced by contaminated plants and will then prove much harder to eliminate. Suitable treatments for plants can be obtained from most pet stores. Provided the instructions for usage are followed carefully, no harm will come to the plants.

The colorful koi stands out in this pond with a dark background. To preserve swimming space for fish, keep plant growth in check by regular pruning of shoots and roots.

OXYGENATING PLANTS

These are potentially most at risk from being allowed to dry out, since they are generally found under water, although some produce flowers above the water's surface. Oxygenating plants, popularly described as oxygenators, do not have to be set in containers. Like most truly aquatic plants, their roots are used more for anchorage than for the uptake of nutrients, which are absorbed directly through the leaves. Oxygenators are typically sold in bunches lacking roots. This is quite usual and need not be a cause for concern, since they will soon develop roots in the pond.

Oxygenators are especially valuable in a new pond, since they will establish themselves rapidly, before other plants such as water-lilies, and utilize the nutrients present in solution, thus helping to prevent an overgrowth of algae, which can be harmful as well as unsightly. Oxygenators are certainly not among the most attractive aquatic plants, but they are essentially functional. If conditions are too favorable for them, thinning is likely to be

Pistia *(water lettuce)* and Salvinia *are attractive floating plants, but they can turn into undesirable weeds in the garden pond. Under certain climatic conditions they grow very fast and are known to choke aquatic life in natural waterways.*

required. Many can survive quite well in relatively shady surroundings, although oxygenators generally tend to favor well-lighted conditions. They are relatively unperturbed by the presence of fountains and waterfalls but will be moved about by the prevailing currents unless they are rooted in position.

Ceratophyllum demersum.

Ceratophyllum demersum: Popularly known as coontail, this plant is also called hornwort. Its fine leaves contribute to its tail-like appearance, forming thick, dark green whorls around a central stem. Coontail will survive well in relatively shady surroundings. As the growing season progresses it tends to break up, with the younger tips of the shoots falling to the bottom of the pond. Here they remain dormant over the winter, establishing a root system during the following spring and then repeating the whole process.

Elodea canadensis: A very popular member of its genus in aquatic circles, the Canadian pondweed is a hardy native plant of North America. It is a vigorous grower that on occasion may need to be curtailed by being thinned out. Shoots can be rooted easily simply by being weighed down in a suitable container.

Some confusion exists over the scientific classification of this group of plants. Approximately ten distinctive species of *Elodea* may occasionally be seen in cultivation, yet

apart from *E. canadensis,*
only goldfish weed is likely
to be encountered with any
degree of regularity, under
the scientific name of
Lagarosiphon major. A
native species of South
Africa, it is a relatively
hardy plant that retains its
attractive green coloration
throughout the year. The
leaves are quite small and
slightly curved, arranged at
short distances along the
full length of the stem.
These plants are very
straightforward to cultivate
and need very little
attention. *Elodea* was once
replaced by the generic
name *Anacharis,* resulting
in the common name
anacharis for elodea
species.

Fontinalis: An ideal
subject for a relatively dull
and shady part of a pond,
willow moss will create an
attractive appearance,
especially in relatively clear
water when its moss-like
growth form can be seen
from above. It readily
establishes itself on rocks
and even the sides of the
pond, but it is unlikely to
create problems by
excessive growth. Moving
water will not disturb
willow moss, so it can be
useful in a pond with a
fountain.

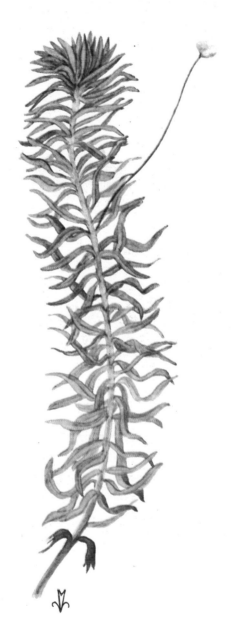

Elodea densa, another popular
water plant for aquariums and
ponds.

Hottonia palustris.

Myriophyllum *photographed in its natural habitat in the Amazon.*

Hottonia palustris: This plant is named water violet as a result of Its purplish mauve flowers, which are evident extending as much as 10 inches into the air on green stems. After flowering, the water violet undergoes a change in appearance, parts of the plant breaking away from the central mass and sinking to the floor of the pond. Here they remain dormant until the next spring. Water violet will not do well unless it is kept in still waters. A related species, *Hottonia inflata,* can be recognized by its air-filled stems, which are swollen in appearance and assist the plant's buoyancy.

Myriophyllum spicatum: Superficially similar to coontail but distinguishable by its flatter leaf whorls, milfoil is especially valuable in a pond containing fishes as it is a favored spawning site. The feathery appearance of milfoil renders it unsuitable for ponds with a high degree of sediment or algal contamination, as it will soon become clogged with such debris. The flowers of milfoils in general are rather inconspicuous, although they often can be seen above the water level. A red-leaved species of milfoil, *Myriophyllum matogrossense,* tends to be more sensitive to low water temperatures than this species. Another species occasionally advertised is *M. verticillatum,* whose leaves are green. It occurs naturally in both Europe and North America and is quite hardy.

Potamogeton crispus: Described simply as pondweeds, there are both floating and submerged varieties in this genus. *P. crispus* itself, known as curled pondweed because of the shape of its leaves, is an attractive plant, being bronze-green in color. It can be easily distinguished from *P. acutifolius,* which has flat leaves with no serrations evident along their sides.

Proserpinaca palustris: Known as mermaid weed, this plant, another native of North America, can grow either in the air or submersed. In the latter instance its appearance is altered, with its leaves generally being smaller. Flowers invariably are located on stems

Myriophyllum verticillatum.

73

evident above the existing water level.

Ranunculus aquatilis: The water crowfoot is another aquatic plant that produces two distinctive sets of leaves. Those evident on the surface are reminiscent of clovers, with a clear pattern of three lobes evident. The name "crowfoot" reflects its underwater appearance, with the leaves said to bear a resemblance to the foot of a bird, being deeply divided. The color of the small flowers varies according to the species concerned. *R. aquatilis* has white flowers, whereas those of *R. delphinifolius* are yellow. Other members of this genus tend to be found in marshy surroundings rather than under water.

Water hyacinth as it appears in the natural habitat in South America. It is established in many tropical areas where it grows extensively and has become a hazard to navigation in many rivers.

Floating Plants
In common with the oxygenators, this group of plants is directly valuable in curtailing algal growth. They screen the water from sunlight and absorb nutrients directly. Difficulties can arise with floating plants, however, if their growth tends to become too profuse, restricting that of water-lilies for example. This applies notably to the so-called "carpeting" species especially duckweed, but fishes will in fact browse on such vegetation and may help to curb excessive growth.

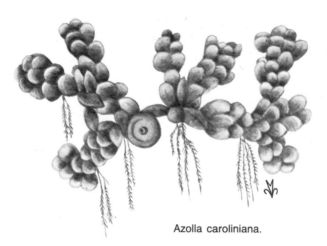

Azolla caroliniana.

Azolla caroliniana: A native species of North America, fairy moss is in fact a form of aquatic fern. In the early part of the year fairy moss forms green aggregates that become reddish later in direct sunlight or as the fall approaches. At the onset of the winter the plants die, with the next generation developing from spores. Growth can be rather slow until the summer, unless the spring is exceptionally mild.

Azolla pinnata, *a species native to Java and Australia that is slightly different from* A. caroliniana.

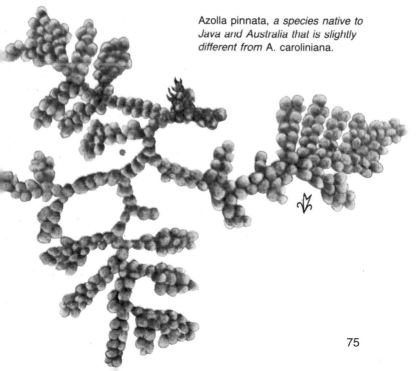

Eichhornia crassipes: The floating water hyacinth grows profusely in the southern United States (where it has been introduced) and has become a serious pest in some areas, clogging up the waterways. It is not a hardy species (being tropical in origin) and is readily killed by frost, so it must be overwintered indoors in more northerly climates. Even so, older plants tend not to prove very viable over this period. The bulbous base of the water hyacinth is full of air, ensuring the plant's buoyancy. Clusters will produce most attractive lilac flowers that are quite striking in appearance. The individual pieces of a cluster can be broken up,

Inflorescence of water hyacinth, Eichhornia crassipes. *Flower color varies according to species.*

with new small sections forming at the base of each part. A blue-flowering species, *E. azurea,* is also sometimes available.

Hydrocharis morsus-ranae: The appearance of this plant, frogbit, is rather reminiscent of a water-lily, especially because of the shape of its leaves. The flowers are white with yellow centers. After the flowering period, however, frogbit dies back. It is the fresh segments that are deposited on the floor of the pond at this stage that ultimately give rise to the plant the following year.

Hydrocharis morsus-ranae.

Lemna trisulca.

Stratiotes aloides: This plant, popularly known as water soldier, is related to frogbit, although they differ significantly in appearance. The water soldier looks rather like the top of a pineapple plant growing in the water. The flowers are white but are distributed differently between male and female plants. Those of the male are arranged in clusters, whereas the flowers of the female are positioned individually. There is no need to worry about obtaining seed in order to propagate this plant, however, as it forms runners that can simply be split off from the parent plant.

Lemna trisucla: Ivy-leafed duckweed is the only duckweed that is really suitable for the pond. It is dark green in appearance and produces inconspicuous flowers that are also green in color. Unlike related species, this duckweed will not spread rapidly to take over the whole surface of the pond. If, however, another species does become established, it may become necessary to skim the surface with a net to remove the surplus at regular intervals.

Trapa natans: The water chestnut is an interesting addition to any pond. Its name comes from the appearance of its seeds, which are black and spiny, rather like those of a chestnut. The seeds are preceded by attractive creamy flowers offset against its green foliage. Water chestnut is an annual plant, with its seeds falling to the bottom of the pond and then germinating during the following spring. Unfortunately, they are susceptible to frost, so in order to ensure that the

Stratiotes aloides.

Gloriosa variety

Rose Arey, cerise pink in color.

following spring and can be returned to the pond once the risk of frost has passed. In this way they will be more advanced than nuts that have survived the winter in the pond and thus can help to contain rapid spread of algae at this time of year.

Water-lilies

This group of plants has long been cherished for their beauty in pond surroundings. As long ago as the eleventh century, Chinese writers were extolling the virtues of the water-lily. The symmetrical shape of the flowers contrasting with their graceful leaves floating on the water's surface reflects only part of their appeal. While there are some 50 natural species of water-lily, many varieties have been produced by selective breeding, giving rise to a wide range of colors from deepest crimson red to yellow and blue to white. The flowers may even be double and can be highly-scented. Indeed, some water-lilies are favored as cut flowers for this reason. (Cut flowers need to be kept in iced water for a period so the blooms will not last only one day, closing at

plants survive from one year to the next it may be necessary to store the nuts in a bowl or dish of water. They must not be allowed to dry out and will need to be kept at a temperature above freezing for the duration of the winter. The nuts should start to germinate during the

Above: *King of Blues.*

Below: *Sunrise, largest variety.*

Above: *Gonnere, also known as Snowball.*

Below: *Maroon Beauty.*

night, but remain open for several days.)

The hybridization and selection that have given rise to the range of colors and petal types have also yielded water-lilies that can be classified on the basis of their planting conditions. Some prove too vigorous for a small pond, whereas others can be grown quite successfully in just a tube of water. It is not possible to document all the water-lilies available, but the following is a representative selection of those that are widely grown and easy to maintain successfully with the minimum of attention.

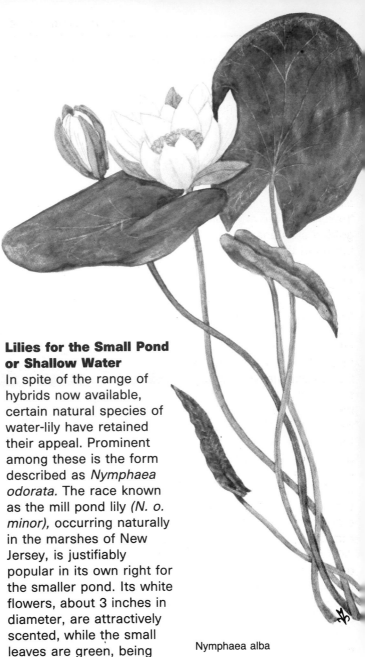

Lilies for the Small Pond or Shallow Water

In spite of the range of hybrids now available, certain natural species of water-lily have retained their appeal. Prominent among these is the form described as *Nymphaea odorata.* The race known as the mill pond lily *(N. o. minor),* occurring naturally in the marshes of New Jersey, is justifiably popular in its own right for the smaller pond. Its white flowers, about 3 inches in diameter, are attractively scented, while the small leaves are green, being reddish on their lower surfaces. This latter feature serves to distinguish this water-lily from the closely-related *N. o. pumila,* which is

Nymphaea alba

characterized by the absence of the reddish underparts to the leaves; instead, they have a purplish tinge.

The *N. pygmaea* hybrids have become very popular for the smaller pond and are available in a range of colors. The white form, described as "alba," should not be confused with the larger common European water-lily, *N. alba.* Its small pure white flowers are offset against golden stamens, and the leaves in this instance are green. A yellow variety of *N. pygmaea,* "Helvola," has mottled leaves with a combination of olive-green and purplish markings. Like other related varieties, "Helvola" is an easy water-lily to cultivate and usually flowers freely. Indeed, blooms can usually be expected within weeks if these water-lilies are planted in a new pond during the spring. Allow for them to spread over an area about 15 inches in diameter. A slightly larger red form, *N. pygmaea* "Rubra," can also be obtained. The flowers in this instance become progressively darker as they mature.

Since the *pygmaea* hybrids require fairly shallow water not exceeding about 12 inches in depth, other forms of water-lily are frequently included even in quite small ponds. These include

Nymphaea pygmaea; *note the small size of this waterlily in comparison to the hand holding one of them.*

the widely cultivated *N. X laydekeri* hybrids, which were developed initially in France and served to establish the popularity of water-lilies in water-gardening circles. A profusion of colors can now be obtained in this case, with the likely use of the white *N. tetragona* in the ancestry of this group being reflected by *N. X laydekeri* "Alba." The yellow stamens create a

Some waterlily varieties.

Marliac Rosea

Gladston

Chromatella

powerful odor rather reminiscent of fresh tea. One of the most prolific varieties in this group is "Purpurata." Under favorable conditions it will flower consistently from early spring until the frost returns. The blooms are deep purplish red with orangish offset against green leaves which have purplish undersides. *N.* X *laydekeri* "Fulgens" is another reddish variety,

this one highly scented; its flowers are crimson in color. It is one of the older hybrids, in existence by 1895.

This group of lilies was named by their creator, Joseph Marliac, after his son-in-law, Maurice Laydeker. Some change in color as the flowers mature, as in perhaps the most striking member of this group, *N.* X *laydekeri* "Lilacea." The flowers in

84

Escarboucle

Rose Arey

this instance are pink when they first open and turn reddish crimson over the course of several days. The petals themselves create an attractive contrast with the bright yellow stamens.

Another group of hybrids developed by Marliac are more suitable for slightly larger ponds, being strong-growing and equally easy to cultivate, although their actual origins have been lost. *N. X. marliacea* water-lilies will thrive in the deeper areas of the average pond, requiring a depth of at least 18 inches of water. A traditional cultivar of this hybrid is *N. X. marliacea* "Chromatella," one of the most striking of all the yellow water-lilies, with its flowers being offset against the attractive mottled appearance of its leaves. One of the most

"Ignea" is a deeper shade of red, bordering on crimson. The flowers are large, and individually they may have a diameter of 6 inches or so. The blooms themselves are relatively upright and rather reminiscent of tulips in shape. Another deep red variety is "Flammea," which won an award of merit in 1897, shortly after its introduction to the water-gardening scene. In this instance the flowers are actually flecked with white markings, with the outer petals being paler.

Water-lilies for the Large Pond

The most spectacular forms of water-lilies, those with the biggest flowers, may prove unsuitable for the average pond. *Nymphaea* "Sunrise," for example may spread 3 feet over the surface and needs equally deep water conditions if it is to thrive. The depth of coloration of this rich golden water-lily is probably unsurpassed, while the individual blooms can be as much as 10 inches in diameter. "Sunrise" has predominantly greenish leaves and the stems are covered in a layer of hairs.

One of the most notable of Marliac's individual

On account of overcrowding, the floating leaves of a waterlily will extend above water seeking greater exposure to sunlight.

vigorous of the *marliacea* hybrids is "Carnea," which has a powerful vanilla scent. The color of the flowers in this instance is variable, ranging from almost pure white in the case of recently planted water-lilies of this variety to a pale shade of pink in established plants.

creations is the striking hybrid christened "Escarboucle." This water-lily, with huge crimson flowers sometimes measuring 12 inches across, combines both depth of coloration and fragrance. The appearance of the flowers is further enhanced by the golden stamens, which serve to emphasize the color of the petals themselves.

Tropical Water-lilies

While all these water-lilies are hardy, a further wide selection can be grown in mild localities out of doors. They can be broadly divided into two categories on the basis of their flowering habits. Some of these so-called "tropical" water-lilies will bloom during the day, whereas others flower only after dark, although they may remain open on cloudy days as well. The night-flowering group are often popular as cut flowers because of their stout stems and fragrance.

OTHER HARDY FLOATERS

Some hardy plants resembling water-lilies can also occasionally feature on dealers' lists, of which the pond lilies or nuphars are most commonly seen.

When grown under ideal conditions, waterlily leaves lie flat on the water's surface as seen here.

The dwarf pond lily (*Nuphar pumila*) is the best species, since it does not require any great depth of water if it is to flourish, being content when submerged to a depth of just 12 inches. The flowers are certainly not as striking as those of a water-lily, although they are bright yellow and projected on rigid stems above the

Nymphoides peltata.

peltata), which has yellow flowers resembling those of buttercups, and golden club (Orontium aquaticum). The latter is in fact a very versatile plant that can be used either as a marginal or in deeper water. The green foliage floats on the water's surface, through which the bright yellow flowers on white stems protrude. These are narrow and spikey in appearance and are often produced in profusion.

MARGINAL PLANTS

While some marginals are cultivated essentially for their decorative appearance, others are valued because of their flowers. The marsh marigolds (Caltha species) are prominent in the latter group, partly because they rank among the earliest plants to flower in the spring. The appearance of their bright yellow flowers is a sign that life is stirring within the pond after the winter. Various species of marsh marigold can be obtained. The common form (C. palustris) is similar in appearance to a buttercup whose appearance has been refined in the cultivar "Flore-pleno" to yield double blooms. A white variety has also been

water level. The leaves are similar in shape. These plants are best displayed in a relatively informal setting.

Water hawthorn (Aponogeton distachyus) is also well worth considering for inclusion in the deeper parts of the pond. It flowers freely from spring to fall and has a delightful vanilla fragrance. The blooms themselves are white, contrasting with the black stamens in the center of each flower.

Other plants in this category include water fringe (Nymphoides

established but is not especially popular compared with its yellow counterpart. This form, "Alba," is also more prone to disease and harder to cultivate successfully.

Marsh marigolds generally grow well and are relatively adaptable. They can even be featured successfully in a bog garden. While most forms do not often exceed 18 inches in height, the biggest species, *C. polypetala,* can grow to double this size and is best reserved for the borders of bigger ponds.

The inclusion of water forget-me-not *(Myosotis scorpioides)* alongside marsh marigolds can be recommended in order to create an attractive contrast. In a late spring they may flower almost simultaneously, with the blue color of the forget-me-not set against that of the marsh marigold. The aquatic form is in fact a richer blue than its better-known counterpart and tends to flower over a longer period. It can be easily raised from seed.

Later in the year, a variety of marginal plants can be relied upon to introduce color to the poolside. The iris is a plant that does well in damp

Oriontium aquaticum.

Acorus calamus.

Sweet flag (A. calamus) is prominent among the marginals most highly valued for their foliage. Its leaves are similar to those of irises but vary in color. The natural form is green, but an ornamental cultivar, "Variegatus," has its leaves edged with pale cream markings. Occasionally other forms are available, including A. gramineus, which is a dwarf variety not exceeding 12 inches in height.

The flowering rush (Butomus umbellatus) has leaves that are rather like swords in appearance. They are red at first, turning green as they mature. The flowers are rose-pink in color and produced in the later part of the year. They are not especially striking, although the flowering rush is an attractive plant in any event.

Many people want to include bulrushes in their pond, but in reality they are actually thinking of cattails (Typha species), with the swollen brown fluffy ends to their flower spikes. The giant cattail (T. latifola) is generally too big and invasive for the average pond, but smaller species are available and can prove appealing. The dwarf Japanese form (T. minima) is well worth considering. It has the typical appearance of the group but does not grow much beyond 18 inches in height. A slightly larger form is often advertised as T. laxmanni.

The bulrush itself (Scirpus lacustris) is not especially striking in comparison, but several cultivars have been developed. These can be variegated, as in the case of the zebra rush ("Zebrinus"). The leaves in this instance are green and cream in color. Not all of these forms are hardy, and if the winter weather is likely to be harsh, they are best removed from the pond and stored where the temperature will not fall low enough to give rise to a frost.

One poolside plant, the skunk cabbage *(Lysichitum americanum),* actually produces its yellow flowers, which resemble those of the arum lily *(Calla* species), before its decorative leaves. These can grow to 30 inches. The plant is named after its similarity to cabbage leaves combined with a pungent aroma. It is attractive and hardy. This particular species produces seeds that germinate well when planted in damp soil, but it is more usually propagated from rootstock divided in early spring.

Waterlily leaf that is heavily infested with aphids.

CHOOSING PLANTS

Your supplier may well have other pond plants available. Since they are usually sold with culturing instructions, they should not be difficult to establish successfully. Avoid purchasing any plants that appear sickly, however, with their leaves being yellow or showing other evident sign of disease.

Various diseases of water-lilies are well-recognized. Aphids can attack the leaves, soon rendering them unsightly. Wipe them off as soon as possible if they appear. A population of these pests can overwinter on plum and cherry trees, so these should be sprayed routinely to break the aphid's life-cycle. Other points to look for when purchasing water-lilies are any signs of disfigurement of the leaves, notably with abnormal leaf spots, bearing in mind that some varieties are more mottled than others. There is no real treatment available, although the plants themselves will not be harmed by this disease. In contrast, water-lily root rot can destroy water-lilies, and thus all lilies should be inspected carefully prior to purchase to ensure that they are alive.

PLANTING

It is usually best to set all the plants for the pond in separate containers rather than attempting to allow them to establish themselves at liberty in the pond. This can have potentially damaging effects, especially on a pond liner. Containers should serve to contain the growth of the more invasive plants such as bur reed *(Sparganium ramosum)*, preventing sharp rhizomes from penetrating the liner on the base of the pond.

Plant containers for the garden pond, ordinary clay pot and plastic latticed type.

Special containers for pond use are available in various sizes, depending on the purpose for which they are required. It is important to avoid overcrowding the pond with plants from the outset, so it will not become totally choked at a later date. Some pond-keepers recommend allowing just one water-lily and one marginal plant in a pond for every 2.4 square yards of surface area.

94

In any event, the key is to allow some clear areas of water to remain, even if you do not intend to include fishes in the pond. Follow the planting instructions that came with the plants and plan accordingly, based on the cultivation details, such as the likely spread of the water-lilies at the surface.

PREPARING THE CONTAINERS

The containers now used for water plants have latticed sides and are relatively broad, providing adequate support for tall plants such as irises that would otherwise prove unstable if they were set in a more conventional pot. The free circulation of water through the holes assists in establishing the plants.

No special soil is required to grow water plants successfully, although it is best to avoid using manure and similar composts with a high level of organic matter, as this will simply encourage algal growth. The high level of nutrients will be taken up by algae, which can then multiply rapidly.

First line the container with a layer of burlap and then sieve the soil to remove the coarse debris.

The burlap is sold by most pond suppliers and serves to prevent the soil being washed out through the holes of the container once it is submerged. The plant should then be set in the soil, following the planting instructions. Remove any dead leaves carefully beforehand, since these will simply decompose in the pond.

It is preferable to set all the plants in containers, even oxygenators. These can simply be buried in groups and weighed down in the soil with their lead collars still attached. Never

A Nymphaea *species in its natural habitat in Brazil.*

leave the collars exposed, since the plants will rot away below them and then float freely around the pond. The lead strip can of course be removed before planting, in which case the oxygenators will have to be carefully weighed down with a stone, taking care not to actually crush the stems or introduce limestone of any form to the pond by this means. A pencil is a useful planting tool for oxygenators.

Water-lilies differ in the way that they must be planted, depending upon the variety concerned. This is essentially a reflection of the shape of their rootstock. Those of the *Nymphaea odorata* group have horizontal corms and are planted accordingly, being simply buried flat with a shallow covering of soil. In contrast, water-lilies that have roots emanating from all sides of the crown, such as *N. X. marliacea* and related forms, are set vertically, leaving the crown uncovered. *N. X. laydekeri* may be positioned at slightly more of an angle in the soil, in contrast to *N. X. marliacea.*

Place a thick layer of coarse lime-free gravel on

*Suggested equipment and plantings for garden pond.*Clockwise from bottom: *air pump, limestone to neutralize acid water, potted plants, garden hose for conveying water to replace water lost through evaporation.*

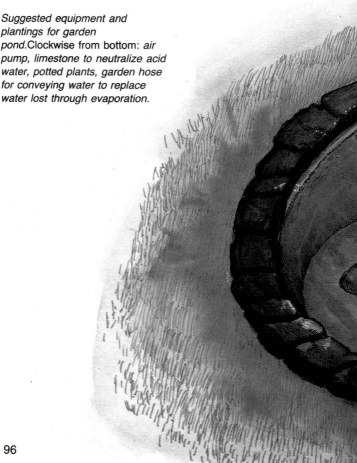

top of the soil once the lilies or other plants have been firmed into the soil. This will help to prevent the soil being washed away, especially when the container is first submerged. It will also protect the plants from fishes that may attempt to burrow into the substrate seeking particles of food.

PLACING THE CONTAINERS IN THE POND

In the first instance, irrespective of the final depth of the container within the pond, it should be lowered slowly onto the marginal shelf so that the air in the soil can be forced out to the surface. It is preferable to leave water-lilies here until they show signs of life, producing new leaves, when they can then be lowered into the main body of water. The likelihood of their rotting is reduced once they have actually started to produce leaves. Oxygenators, in

contrast, can be lowered without any problem once their container is water-logged.

While the central area of the pond is likely to be the deepest part, it is still possible to include marginals such as irises here if desired. Simply place the container on a firm base at the appropriate depth below

Waterlily seeds are cleaned before planting in a commercial nursery. In the wild, waterlily seeds fall to the bottom and germinate directly.

the water's surface.

Depending on the construction of the pond, it may be possible to set plants directly into the base, but this is not to be recommended even in natural ponds. Some plants become very invasive if unrestrained by a container, and their

growth can then be very difficult to curtail. It is also easier to divide plants if they are set in containers. This applies especially to many of the marginal plants, such as irises, marsh marigolds, and most foliage plants.

PROPAGATION OF POND PLANTS

The younger shoots around the outside of a root mass are likely to prove the most vigorous, and these can be set in separate containers. If you have a surplus of marginal plants, you may be able to transfer some to a damp corner of the garden, depending on the species concerned. They may establish themselves successfully there, provided the roots are not allowed to dry out at any stage.

Water-lilies are propagated by slightly different means. Some, notably *N. pygmaea* "Alba," need to be grown directly from seed. This should be sown in a pan of sieved garden soil, which is kept just covered with water. The seed is very susceptible to dehydration and must be sown as soon as possible after collection or kept moist. Germination may take two weeks or so.

The young water-lilies can then be destroyed by algae, notably the filamentous form, which serves to clog up the tiny seedlings. Chemical control of the algae is possible if this problem occurs. Keep the seedlings immersed in water throughout; ultimately they can be moved to bigger containers. A fish tank partially filled with water can be useful for this purpose.

Alternatively, you may be able to divide the water-lily into two if it has become overgrown. Under these circumstances the root mass may actually split open a plastic container. The individual parts of the plant can then be set in separate containers, with the roots being cut back slightly if necessary. The best time to undertake this task is in the spring, so the divided portions should establish themselves rapidly.

At this time it may also be possible to take off some "eyes" from the roots themselves. The "eyes" are in fact dormant shoots that can be cut off and planted separately, while the parent plant may be divided if required. Treat with charcoal any open cuts that could be

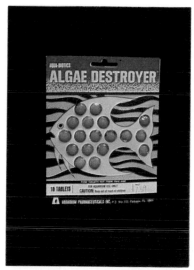

Algicides can be used to clear undesirable algal growth on seeds and seedlings.

attacked by fungus; this will be safe for any fishes in the pond. Proprietary treatments can be used for water-lilies kept apart from fishes, but some may prove toxic if introduced into the pond. Check on this before use. The planted eyes should be kept in a suitable container and covered with water. The depth of water will need to be increased as the plants grow. It is likely to take a couple of years or longer before they are large enough to flower.

Some tropical water-lilies, in contrast to hardy types, can be propagated from plantlets that develop on their leaves close to the stem. Under these

Although the banana plant (Nymphoides) survives submerged in fish tanks, it will only propagate out of doors in direct sunlight.

circumstances, simply cut off the whole leaf and transplant it to a small perforated container that will ultimately be submerged in water. Here the plantlet will develop roots and must be kept fully immersed.

Acrylic fish tanks are the most suitable containers for water-lilies, being relatively light to carry compared with glass aquaria. Additional lighting can be supplied by using a natural daylight tube in a hood of the appropriate size. Lights of this type are thought to encourage plant growth and thus are of special value for propagation purposes.

While the cultivation of water-lilies by such means is likely to be a prolonged process, it is nevertheless very satisfying when the first flowers develop on your rootstock.

A pond is guaranteed to open new areas of interest for the keen gardener, whether dividing the plants within the pond or selecting suitable plants to place around its perimeter. The choice in this latter instance is immense, but again, thought should be given to providing interest and color throughout the year. Primulas of various species and irises can be incorporated to provide flowers, while ferns and other moisture-loving plants will add attractive foliage. There is considerable scope, especially with ferns of many different sizes being available. Some will make an attractive back-drop for the scene, whereas others are sufficiently small to be featured alongside low-growing plants at the front of the pond without proving obtrusive.

Plants that provide ground cover, such as creeping Jenny or loosestrife *(Lysimachia nummularia)*, should also be considered, possibly alongside taller plants in order to reduce to a minimum the amount of weeding required. This particular plant remains green throughout most of the year and bears rich golden flowers during the summer. It may even spread into the water, where it will develop roots, and can break away, establishing itself on the bottom as an oxygenator, although no flowers will be produced in these surroundings. Plants of this type can also be especially valuable in a rock garden alongside small, early-flowering plants such as snowdrops and alpines that are ideally displayed under such conditions.

Above: Lysimachia nummularia *is available in most aquarium shops.*

Below: *Open holes indicate that some sort of pest is destroying the leaves of your waterlilies. Turn over the leaf to expose the culprits.*

Fishes and Others

For most people, a pond is incomplete unless it features some type of fish. Fishes form part of the natural scenery and can actually prove beneficial within the environment. Their excrement will be broken down by bacteria via the nitrogen cycle to yield nitrate, which in turn is used by the plants as a

A goldfish with fungus on the body.

fertilizer. The fish will also feed on invertebrates such as mosquito larvae in the pond and actively reduce the number of midges that may otherwise emerge from the depths of the pond.

The key to maintaining fishes successfully in a garden pond is to not overstock the environment, remembering that the fishes will grow well if conditions are favorable and they then will require more space. Never add new fishes directly to an established pond in case they are carrying parasites or other diseases, since once established it may prove very difficult to eradicate such problems without actually draining the pond and then restocking it.

CHOOSING FISHES

The best time to purchase fishes is in the late spring or early summer so that they have adequate opportunity to become established and feed well before the onset of winter. When assessing fishes, avoid any that swim at an abnormal angle in the water or that show clear signs of fin damage. Any evident injury, or ulceration of the body is a serious and possibly life-threatening condition for the fish.

Look for an active and vigorous fish with clear eyes. A "halo" appearance on the body may be indicative of a fungal infection. White spots on a fish can be caused by a parasitic disease, but in the case of goldfish, similar markings on the gill covers and spreading along the pectoral fins are characteristic of male fish in breeding condition. This in fact is the best means of recognizing the sex of these popular pond occupants. Females in spawning condition may

appear rather swollen because of the presence of eggs in their bodies. They will be a source of attraction for males, which will repeatedly nudge their sides and may actively chase them around the tank.

Keep a watchful eye on the condition of your fish. Sick and overaged fish should be culled regularly.

STOCKING THE POND

The size of the fishes chosen will have a direct bearing on their price. Clearly, there is much to be said for obtaining relatively small fishes and growing them out within

Your newly purchased fish can be acclimated into the pond using the original plastic bag, or quarantine the fish in a small aquarium for a few days.

the confines of the pond. Larger fishes will certainly be older, and although they may attempt to breed before their smaller counterparts, they can

prove less adaptable and have a shorter life span in the pond. Goldfish and koi, the most popular occupants of garden ponds, are quite long-lived, though, with a likely life expectancy of a decade or more.

Having decided on the fishes, do not exceed a stocking density of 2 inches of fish for every square foot of water. This rule is based on surface area of the pond, since this is where the water and atmospheric oxygen are in contact. Overstocking is liable to lead to an oxygen shortage for the fishes, causing them to gulp repeatedly at the surface, especially during hot weather. Also make an allowance for the growth of the fishes, since once liberated into a pond and well-fed they will grow rapidly.

The plants will take several weeks to become really established, so it is preferable for this reason alone not to immediately introduce fishes into a new pond. The dangers of free lime and chlorine must also be considered. There is an additional reason for keeping the fishes out of the pond for a week or so after they are acquired: You will be able to check that all are eating well and do not appear ill. Any parasites that can be easily seen can be treated at this stage rather than introducing such problems to the pond.

Therefore, purchase an acrylic aquarium of suitable size and a dechlorinator so that the fishes can be transferred safely to the tank immediately after it has been set up. It is advisable to float the plastic bag in which the fishes will have been sold on top of the water in the tank for 20 minutes or so (having added the dechlorinator in the first instance) before liberating them. This will ensure that the water in the bag and the aquarium will be of about equal temperatures so the fishes will not be suddenly exposed to widely differing water temperatures, as could otherwise occur. Although not necessarily harmful, this will be stressful for the fishes and could encourage an outbreak of disease. Similarly, they should be transferred to the pond in an identical fashion for the same reason.

Should you suspect that any of the fishes are ailing, you can obtain various commercial remedies from

A dip net with a strong frame and handle is indispensable equipment for a garden pond keeper. A set of several sizes can not be considered superfluous.

your local pet store to treat the conditions. These will probably have to be diluted as directed, and ideally the affected fish should be kept in a separate tank. Use a well-padded net when catching a fish so as not to injure the scales, and avoid handling a fish directly, as this can also damage its protective body covering. Wet hands will minimize the risk of such an injury, but the fish will prove very slippery under these circumstances. Having caught the fish in a net, the safest means of transferring it elsewhere is to leave it in the net, just covering the top with a wet hand so that it cannot jump out.

FEEDING

It is important not to overfeed fishes, especially while they are still in a quarantine tank, since excess food will just pollute the water. When in a pond, fishes are most commonly fed a specially prepared pelleted diet that they will supplement with other items such as insect larvae. The main

In addition to the popular pelleted form, garden pond fish food is also available in flake form.

advantage of using a pelleted food is that it floats, and the fishes will thus be attracted to the surface to feed. Some can become very tame, especially if they are fed at the same time every day so that it becomes a routine.

Pellets also can be used quite adequately while the fishes are in the tank. Never feed more than are eaten within a few minutes of being offered. It is better to offer just a small quantity several times during the day. Fishes do of course feed for much of the day and will not tend to eat a large amount at one time.

Keeping the fishes in an aquarium for any length of time means that the water may need to be partially changed at intervals. If you use a siphon, the required volume (about one third

One of the enjoyments of having a garden pond, feeding your favorite fish by hand.

every two weeks) can be removed easily. The fresh water should be left to stand for at least half an hour, with the dechlorinator added, before being cautiously added to the tank. In this way there should again be no great variation in temperature between the two volumes of water.

A school of goldfish enjoying their food ration.

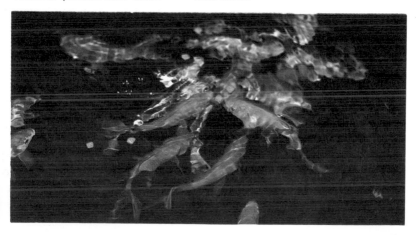

RELEASING THE FISHES

Another advantage of leaving the pond empty for several weeks is that water-lilies should have grown to the surface. Their leaves will provide cover for fishes faced with several potential predators in their new environment. Some cats can be a persistent problem around

died, although bodies are never seen. Occasionally though, a large fish may be severely injured, being impaled by a heron with its beak yet not actually removed from the pond, and this will tend to confirm the culprit.

While special netting to cover the water can be acquired, this does nothing

The common goldfish is a beginner's garden pond fish. They are colorful, inexpensive, and easy to keep.

a pond, harassing the occupants and injuring them, often fatally, even if they cannot catch them. The other major danger may be less evident. Herons frequently descend and remove fishes from the pond in the early morning, so they may not even be seen. The owner simply assumes the fishes

to enhance the appearance of the pond. It should be suspended off the surface so that there is no risk of the fishes injuring themselves by jumping against the mesh. Koi can be especially bad in this regard.

GOLDFISH

A member of the carp family, the goldfish *(Carassius auratus)* appears to have first been developed in China as long

Above: *Veiltail goldfish, a variety best kept in display tanks in the home, not in a garden pond.*

Below: *Bubble-eyed or celestial goldfish, another goldfish variety that is quite unsuited for a garden pond.*

ago as 800 A.D. Since then, well over 100 varieties have emerged, although some remain scarce and not all are suitable to be kept in ponds throughout the year. This applies especially to those varieties with elaborate finnage, such as the veiltail. Apart from being more at risk from fin rot caused by less than ideal water conditions, goldfish of this type are also likely to suffer from severe fin congestion during cold weather. These goldfish have a relatively corpulent body shape and are less active than their more streamlined counterparts, such as the comet. This variety was

Blackmoor goldfish, chosen by some for color contrast in their pond.

developed toward the end of the last century in the United States and is characterized by its deeply forked tail fin. Although it has been bred in various colors, the red and white form christened the "Sarasso comet" has become the most popular.

Apart from differences in body shape, mutations affecting the scales of the goldfish have also occurred. This in turn has altered the colors of the fish, with the reflective cells beneath the scales being affected. The London shubunkin is described as the nacreous form of the normal goldfish, simply because these cells, known as iridocytes, are fewer in number. The markings in this instance are frequently bluish offset against orange and white markings, creating a blotched appearance. The Bristol shubunkin differs slightly in that its fins are more highly developed, but daily through the warmer months of the year. Lengths of 10 inches or so are not uncommon under favorable conditions. It is of course possible to keep the more sensitive varieties out of doors just for the summer, bringing them indoors for the duration of the winter. Those with highly developed eyes, such as the bubble-eye,

London shubunkin goldfish, well-known variety kept in garden ponds world-wide.

it is otherwise similar in appearance to its London counterpart. These fish are now bred in huge numbers on a worldwide basis.

While goldfish kept indoors in aquaria may not grow to their full potential, those living in ponds will grow rapidly, provided that they are fed several times are probably best excluded from the pond environment since they are liable to be injured under these conditions. The more brightly colored fish are more likely to show up well. The black Moor, although an impressive fish in the aquarium, contrasting well with its more colorful relatives, proves relatively inconspicuous in the average pond.

KOI

The koi is another member of the family Cyprinidae, like the goldfish, and can grow to at least 20 inches, although this size may not be attained in most garden ponds. Koi are truly spectacular fish of great beauty in many cases. They really need to be kept in quite spacious surroundings and are likely to damage plants included in their pool.

Koi appear to have been developed in Japan from the common carp *(Cyprinus carpio),* which is rather a dull fish popular for food. A wide range of colors and color combinations has now been developed, and these are still described under Japanese names, although these ornamental carp are being bred on an increasing scale in the United States and elsewhere. Top quality show specimens command extremely high prices when they change hands.

The red form is described as *Aka Muji,*

Expert koi breeders, mostly Japanese, can identify the many varieties by sight.

Above: *A group of the golden variety of koi, called* Ohgon, *tame enough to submit to petting.*

Below: *The red form of koi,* Aka Muji.

with the golden koi, *Ohgon,* also being very popular. Space does not permit a detailed breakdown of the colors of the koi here, but these can be found in other more specialized titles, notably *Koi of the World* by Dr. Herbert R. Axelrod.

OTHER FISHES

Whereas carp by nature tend to be bottom-feeders, as shown by the sensory barbels present around the koi's mouth, some other pond fishes frequent the upper areas of water. Probably the most notable of these is the golden orfe *(Idus idus),* which is a rich golden color, although there is also a duller silver form. Orfe readily seek insects that venture too close to the water's surface, often leaping out for this reason. They will not thrive in sluggish, poorly oxygenated water and thus are quite at home in a pond containing a fountain. Orfe are shoaling fish by nature and really need to be kept in small groups rather than individually. They can be housed quite successfully alongside goldfish of similar size if desired.

Various other fishes may sometimes be included in a garden pond but are certainly not as colorful or popular as the preceding species. They include species of catfish, which are secretive fishes often inhabiting more sluggish water. Although foragers by nature, they can also prove actively predatory, especially toward young fry.

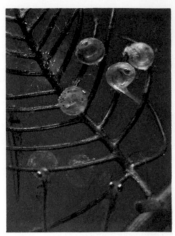

Above: *These goldfish eggs are ready to hatch. Note a newly hatched fish resting at the bottom.*

Below: *Dead goldfish eggs appear opaque and are attacked by fungus.*

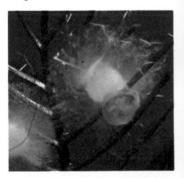

BREEDING GOLDFISH IN POND SURROUNDINGS

When goldfish are housed in a pond, their keeper has less control over their breeding habits than if they were housed in an aquarium. Nevertheless, under these more natural conditions there is an increased likelihood that a proportion of the fry will

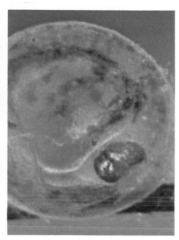

Above: *Closeup of goldfish egg with live embryo seen clearly.*

Below: *Brine shrimp nauplii, live food for goldfish fry.*

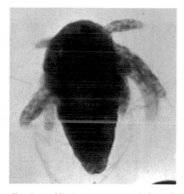

relentlessly, bringing themselves sometimes almost to the point of total exhaustion. At this time fish tend to lose their natural caution and are more at risk from predators such as cats. External fertilization of the eggs takes place, with hatching occurring within a week of egg-laying, although this depends to some extent on the temperature of the water.

In the pond, the fry will be able to obtain their own food, so no supplementary feeding is required. Only a handful are likely to survive, however, so if you want a large number of young fish you will need to rear them in artificial surroundings. You can transfer the spawn from the pond, if you want to hatch it in an aquarium, by simply lifting out the oxygenating plants to which the eggs will have adhered. Under these conditions it is likely that you will be able to rear more of the resulting fry, but this will entail a considerable amount of extra work. A commercial rearing food should be given to the fry once they are free-swimming; later larger items such as brine shrimp nauplii will need to be supplied.

find sufficient natural food and escape their elders.

Goldfish will usually breed for the first time in their second year, attaining maturity by the size of about 3 inches. When the weather warms up in the spring, signs of spawning activity should soon be evident. Males will chase their intended mates

OTHER POND OCCUPANTS

A variety of creatures are likely to be attracted to an established pond. Indeed, for many amphibians the garden pond provides a refuge in the urban environment. Frogs and toads are likely to be most evident, especially in the spring during the mating period. Masses of their spawn will be visible in the water, and these will hatch into tadpoles, provided that the egg mass is not consumed by the fish. Toads *(Bufo)* tend to lay their eggs in long strands, whereas the eggs of the true frogs *(Rana)* form solid clumps. Most anurans, as frogs and toads are collectively

Above: *Although salamanders can survive on land, they have to live very close to water.*

Below: *The giant toad,* Bufo marinus, *found worldwide, is poisonous and other animals avoid eating it.*

described, will not cause any harm in the pond. The bullfrog *(Rana catesbeiana)* and its tadpoles, however, can prove aggressive toward both and other pond occupants. Small fishes may be consumed by these amphibians if they can catch them.

Turtles should be excluded from ponds containing fishes if at all possible: most readily catch and eat small fishes. In addition, the majority of species cannot be kept satisfactorily in garden ponds throughout the year, since they are likely to require deeper water and mud bottoms for winter hibernation or will simply wander away from the pond in search of a more comfortable habitat. Some larger sliders can be kept outside for the duration of the summer if they are not able to escape from the confines of the pond. Bearing in mind that turtles need to be allowed access to land, it will be best to construct a small island in the middle of the pond where they will be able to sun themselves.

Newts prove rather secretive occupants of many ponds, laying and concealing their eggs carefully in masses of oxygenating plants such as

Leopard frog, Rana pipiens, *another well-known species of frog in the United States.*

Elodea. They will not harm the fishes, although occasionally they may catch small fry. As with toads, many newts tend to be largely terrestrial for much of the year outside the breeding season.

A mallard duck may appear nice in a garden pond but they will eat small fish also.

SNAILS AND MUSSELS

The inclusion of snails in a pond is a controversial subject, although once they are present it can be hard to eliminate them. In reality, they may not cause much harm. They are often introduced accidentally via eggs present on plants and may even be brought in on birds' legs. Certain snails, notably the ramshorns (*Planorbis* species), will graze essentially on algae rather than attacking plant life in the pond, and these are to be encouraged.

Freshwater mussels are also included in some ponds. They are filter-feeders and may help to maintain water purity by extracting algae from the water. Mussels actually bury themselves in the substrate of the pond and thus are not entirely suitable for artificial ponds with no floor covering.

Ramshorn snail, Planorbis.

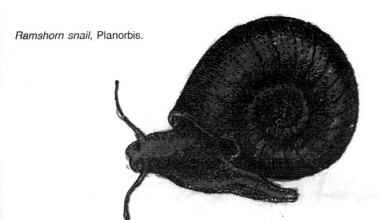

The swan mussel *(Anodonta cygnea)* has a crucial role to play in the breeding of the European fish known as the bitterling *(Rhodcus amarus)*. The female fish lays her eggs in the mussel, where the fry hatch, before exiting via the exhalant siphon of the mussel. The reproductive cycle of this mussel also relies on the fishes, so they can conversely prove disadvantageous in a pond. This is because the immature stage in the mussel's life cycle, described as the glochidia, has to attach itself to a fish and then form a cyst. Here it is nourished for several months before breaking out and establishing itself independently. Although interesting, such mussels are therefore not entirely ideal for ponds containing fishes, unless of course bitterling are also included.

Apple snail, Ampullaria.

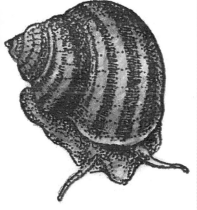

Apple snail eggs laid on a tree trunk in Brazil.

PLANTS

Once established, the pond will need relatively little attention, although at first (and subsequently in each spring) algae can create problems. They will thrive in an environment where plenty of nutrients are available in solution, coupled with abundant sunlight. Dozens of types of alga have been identified in garden ponds. High populations of algae in a pond can remove vital oxygen from the water and may even liberate toxins that will have adverse effects on fishes.

Although chemicals can be used to control "green water," as algal infestations are sometimes described, the best way of curtailing algal growth is by biological means. Once the flowering plants themselves start growing, they will compete with the algae for nutrients and, by spreading and shading the water's surface, will allow less sunlight to penetrate to the main body of the water. As a result, the algae will be starved of nutrients and tend to die out or at least be reduced in numbers.

A more serious problem invariably results from the presence of filamentous algae in the pond. This will

Koi such as this specially bred variety having a golden metallic sheen can be very valuable. They are objects of pride and are exhibited, traded, and sold at very high prices in the Orient. Koi, like goldfish, are able to withstand very low temperatures. However, most garden pond owners in areas where winter is severe usually prefer to have their koi over winter indoors in large aquariums or tanks.

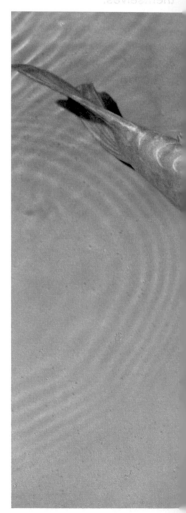

choke other vegetation, forming thick beds. The only effective option under these circumstances is to remove the strands by hand. If left unchecked, this type of algae will spoil the appearance of the pond very rapidly and may harm other plants before they can establish themselves.

In the summer, during dry weather, the level of water in the pond may fall quite rapidly because of evaporation. This loss of water should be made good by using dechlorinated water, taking care to ensure that the temperature of the water used is the same as that in the pond itself.

Left: *A natural channel for draining a garden pond is a big blessing, if present. Think about the hours of work that will be saved in emptying a big garden pond.*

FISHES IN THE WINTER

Adequate preparations must also be made to ensure that the fishes can survive the winter in the pond, otherwise they must be brought indoors as well. This is advisable with goldfish less than 2 inches in overall length as a matter of course. Most hardy fishes in a pond will spend the winter in the deepest portion where the temperature is constant and relatively warm. A minimum depth of 3 feet is usually recommended if you wish to over-winter your fishes.

A garden pond situated in a temperate area will eventually freeze in winter. If fish overwinter in such a pond, be sure air holes are present.

As summer ends, the plants will start to die back. It may be necessary to bring some plants inside for the duration of the winter. This can also ensure that the pond will be planted early the following spring with floating plants that are relatively advanced, thus lessening the likelihood of algal overgrowth at this stage. Plants in the pond will die back naturally at the end of the growing period, but marginals may need to be cut down after flowering. In this instance, ensure that there is no risk of water gaining access to open stems, since this is likely to cause the plant to rot over the winter.

A ball floating on the surface of the pond may help to prevent the water freezing over, but the use of a pond heater is to be recommended. This should certainly keep part of the pond around the heating element free from ice. The heater in most cases will function off the same equipment used to operate the fountain during the summer months. Pond heaters are usually easy to install and highly economical, requiring little electricity as they have a low wattage rating.

The sides of the pond will be under more pressure during the winter since water expands as it freezes. If the pond does start to leak for any reason, the fish will have to be transferred to separate accommodations without delay so that repairs can be carried out. The practicability of this will depend on the individual circumstances, but restoration work must be undertaken carefully, to minimize the risk of further leaks. Silicone sealants can be useful for this purpose within the confines of the pond.

ANOTHER SPRING

In the following spring, the cycle starts again, and the appetite of the fish will return. They should have been fed very judiciously over the winter period. It is unlikely in a newly established pond that the plants will need to be disturbed until the third year at the earliest, by which time they will be well-established. This task needs to be undertaken in the spring.

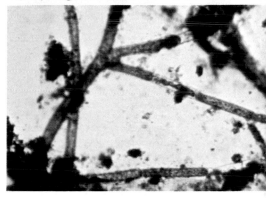

Cladophora, a common green filamentous algae found in natural waterways and ponds.

There should be no need to empty the pond totally under normal circumstances, but temporary drainage may be required if the site is being expanded. A pump connected to a suitable piece of hosing will be ideal for this task and will save a considerable amount of effort in emptying the pond by bailing the water out using buckets.

Suggested Reading

The following books are available in your local pet shops and book shops and T.F.H. Publications, Inc., P.O. Box 427, Neptune, NJ 07753-9989.

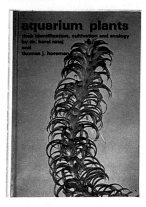

AQUARIUM PLANTS
by Dr. K. Rataj and T. Horeman.
ISBN 0-87666-455-9.
TFH H-966, hardcover. 448 pages, 244 color photos, 124 black and white photos

A complete volume dealing with aquatic plants, including those for the garden pond. Description and methods of propagation are discussed for each species of plant.

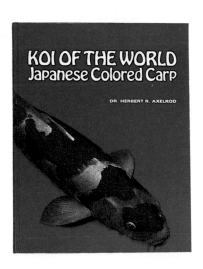

GOLDFISH GUIDE
by Dr. Yoshiichi Matsui.
ISBN 0-87666-545-8
TFH PL-2011, hardcover. 256 pages, 100 color photos, 38 black and white photos, 14 line illustrations.

Contains information on all aspects of the goldfish; its history, types, biology, ecology, diseases, breeding and genetics, by a Japanese author with more than 50 years of academic and practical experience about goldfish.

GOLDFISH AND KOI IN YOUR HOME
by Dr. Herbert R. Axelrod and William Vorderwinkler.
ISBN 0-86622-041-0.
TFH H-909, hardcover. 224 pages, 160 color photos, 20 black and white photos.

Revised edition of a proven popular and useful book on two of the most-kept garden pond fish, the goldfish and the koi.

KOI AND GARDEN POOLS
by Dr. Herbert R. Axelrod.
ISBN 0-86622-398-3
CO-040, hardcover
ISBN 0-86622-399-1 softcover.
128 pages, all photos and illustrations in full color.

Introductory, yet complete, book for anyone ready to keep koi in a garden pool. All aspects about a pool and koi covered.

KOI OF THE WORLD
by Dr. Herbert R. Axelrod.
ISBN 0-87666-092-8.
TFH H-947, hardcover. 239 pages 327 color photos, 22 black and white photos.

Everything a garden pond keeper would like to know about the koi is in this book: varieties of koi, their needs, breeding, disease including sales and exhibiting.

Index

Index
to Plants and Animals

The choice of plants, especially those with flowers, can improve an otherwise ordinary rock garden and pond.

CO-017

A COMPLETE INTRODUCTION TO

GARDEN PONDS

COMPLETELY ILLUSTRATED IN FULL COLOR

This formal garden pool, circular in shape, is worth the cost of construction as an adjunct to a beautiful home.